Windsor Ontario Book 1 in Colour Photos, Saving Our History One Photo at a Time

Photography
by Barbara Raué
2015

Series Name:
Cruising Ontario

Book 117: Windsor - Walkerville

Cover photo: 2088 Willistead Crescent (Page 30)

Series Name: Cruising Ontario
Saving Our History One Photo at a Time
in colour photos

Books Available in Alphabetical Order:
Aberfoyle, Acton, Alton, Ancaster, Arthur, Aylmer, Ayr, Bloomingdale, Brantford, Burlington, Caledon, Caledonia, Cambridge, Clifford, Conestogo, Delhi, Dorchester to Aylmer, Drayton, Drumbo, Dundas, Eden Mills, Elmira, Elora, Fergus, Guelph, Hagersville, Hamilton, Hanover, Harriston, Hespeler, Jarvis, Kitchener, Linwood, Listowel, London, Lucknow, Mono, Mount Forest, Neustadt, New Hamburg, Niagara-on-the-Lake, Oakville, Orangeville, Orillia, Owen Sound, Palmerston, Peterborough, Port Elgin, Preston, Rockwood, Seaforth, Sheffield, Shelburne, Simcoe, Southampton, St. Jacobs, St. Thomas, Stoney Creek, Stratford, Tillsonburg, Waterdown, Waterrford, Waterloo, Wellesley, Wingham

Book 110:Lucknow,Mitchell
Book 111: Conestogo, Bloomingdale
Book 112: Delhi
Book 113: Waterford
Book 114-116: Waterloo
Book 117-119: Windsor

Other Books by Barbara Raue

Coins of Gold

Arrows, Indians and Love

The Life and Times of Barbara
Volume 1: Inventions That Have Enhanced My Life
Volume 2: Entertainment That I Have Enjoyed
Volume 3: East Coast Trips
Volume 4: Olympics Have Always Intrigued Me
Volume 5: Wonders of the World
Volume 6: Caribbean Cruises We Have Enjoyed
Volume 7: Animals
Volume 8: Storms and Other Major Disasters in My Lifetime
Volume 9: Wars, Terrorist Attacks and Major Disasters

The Cromwell Family Book

Laura Secord Discovered

Daddy Where Are You?

Visit Barbara's website to view all of her books
http://barbararaue.ca

Windsor is the southernmost city in Canada. The Detroit River is to the north of the city, which separates it from Detroit, Michigan. Windsor was settled by the French in 1749 as an agricultural settlement. In 1794, after the American Revolution, the settlement of "Sandwich" was founded. It was later renamed Windsor, after the town in Berkshire, England.

Sandwich, Ford City and Walkerville were separate towns until 1935 when they were annexed by Windsor. They remain as historic neighborhoods of Windsor. Walkerville was incorporated as a town in 1890.

The former Town of Walkerville was founded by Hiram Walker in 1858. The New England-born distiller bought two French farms on the south shore of the Detroit River, and the growth of his industry and the town it supported continued for seven decade under his family's guidance.

Railroads played an important part in Walkerville's history. First, the Great Western's extension to Windsor in 1854 opened up opportunities for commercial expansion. Then Walker built his own line in 1885 with government financing, the Lake Erie Essex & Detroit River Railroad, which connected Walkerville with lakeshore towns and farms, and extended as far as St. Thomas. The availability of rail transportation attracted other industrial enterprises to the area, and brought great prosperity to the Walker family and their town.

The Walkerville Land & Building Company was incorporated in 1890 with Hiram's oldest son, Edward Chandler, as president. The Town passed a by-law in 1894 to provide temporary tax exemptions to attract new industries, and to encourage individuals wishing to build homes in Walkerville. Rental properties for the distillery's employees were built. All of the community's amenities were provided by Walker - a fire brigade and police, streetlights, sewers, paved roads and sidewalks, parks, a music hall, a school, library and church.

Walker Road's east side was devoted to industrial manufacturing facilities. Its western edge had modest, brick, semidetached houses; Monmouth Road's semis and terraces replaced rows of cottages, and employees were originally required to rent from the distillery. Argyle Road had a mix of terraces and vernacular houses for a higher rank of employee. Devonshire Road became the main street, with Romanesque Revival semis for management and the clergy. Later, distinctive houses of various architectural styles, popular in the protracted Edwardian Period (1900 to the 1930s), rose on the street, and spilled over onto Kildare Road. The concept was fully realized with the landscaped "island" developed as the site of St. Mary's Anglican Church - the sons' memorial to their parents, and the erection of Willistead Manor on the former Country Club and park lands.

The Arts and Crafts Movement, a philosophy of design founded in England about 1850, emphasized handmade architecture in an age when factory mass-production was taking hold. Every home Albert Kahn designed shows Arts and Crafts influence. Kahn believed that historic period styles were best suited to homes and public institutions, while factories should be utilitarian, brightly illuminated and devoid of ornament.

Table of Contents

Walkerville

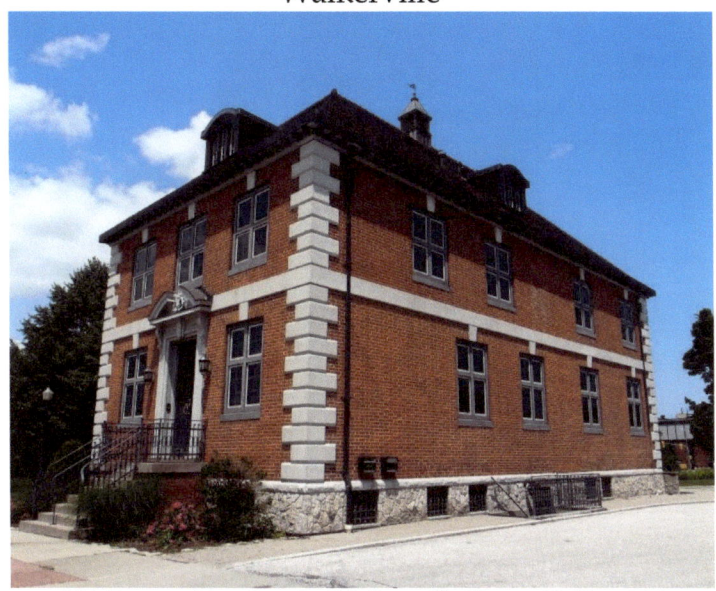

350 Devonshire Road - Walkerville Town Hall - 1904
Classical Revival – symmetrical, belt courses (a continuous row of stones set in the wall), angled quoins, burst pediment above door with coat of arms, dormers, cupola

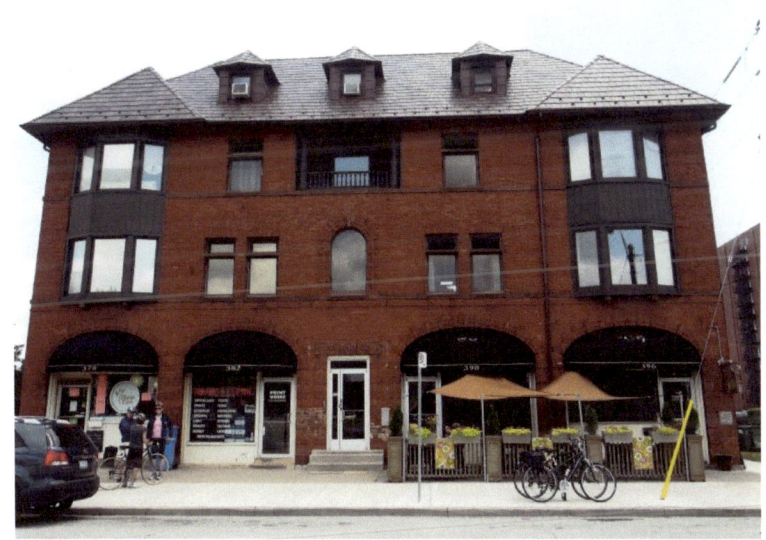

378-396 Devonshire Road - Crown Inn – 1892 – twin gables above oriel windows, three dormers

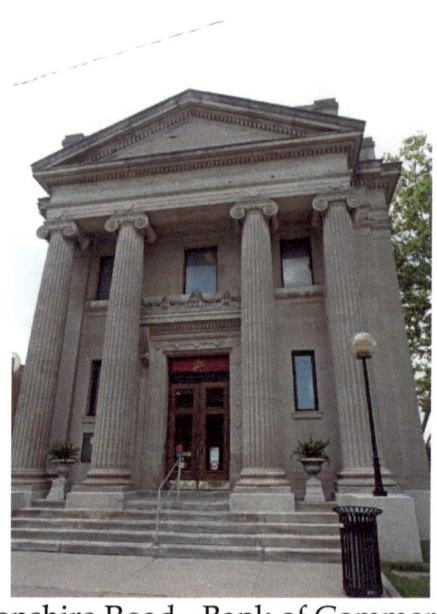

415 Devonshire Road - Bank of Commerce – 1907
Classical Greek, scrolled Ionic capitals on fluted columns, with
a plain pediment above

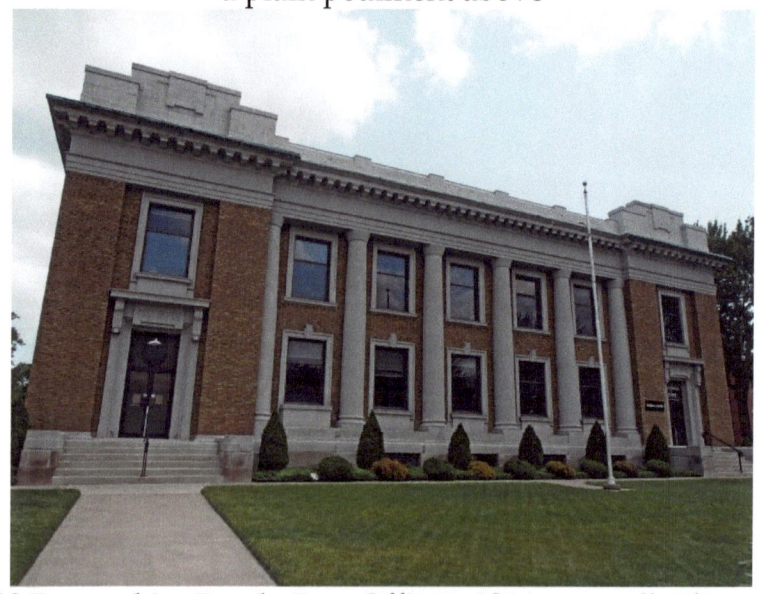

420 Devonshire Road - Post Office – 1914 – six tall pilasters,
rhythmical symmetry

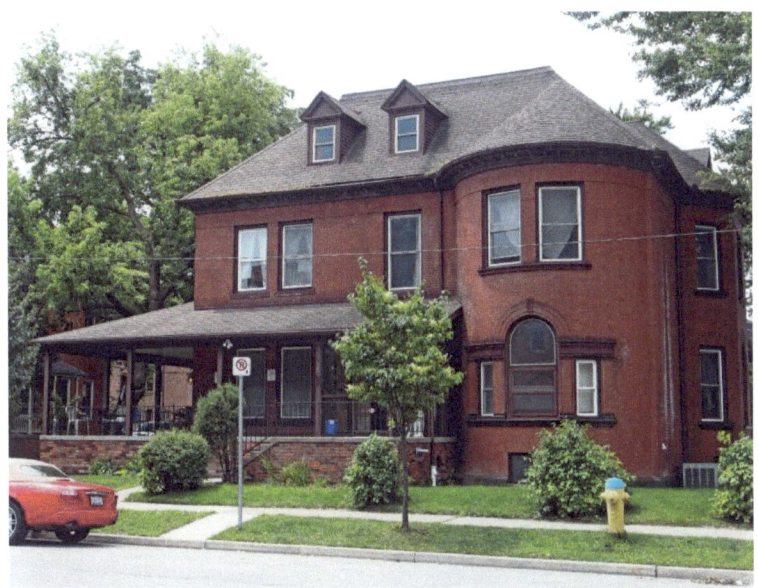

511 Devonshire Road – Thomas Reid House - 1892
Rounded bay with Palladian-style window, dentilled eaves

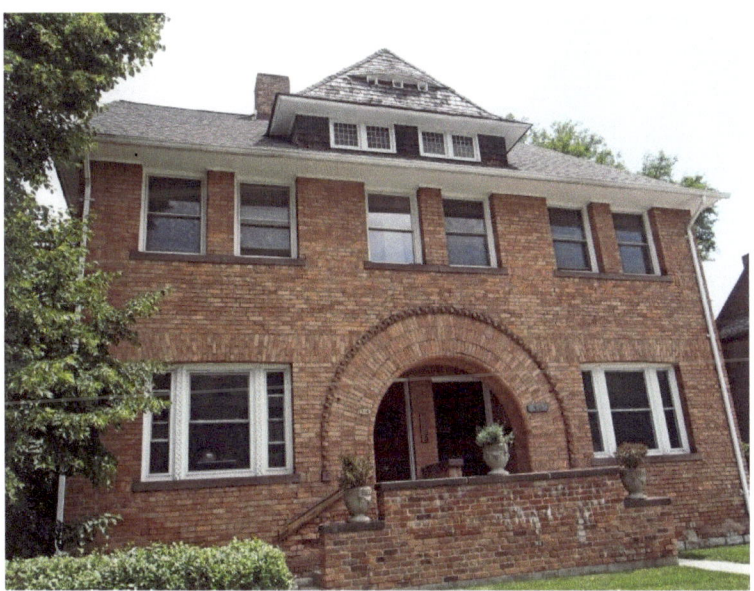

514-516 Devonshire Road – Romanesque style arched entrance

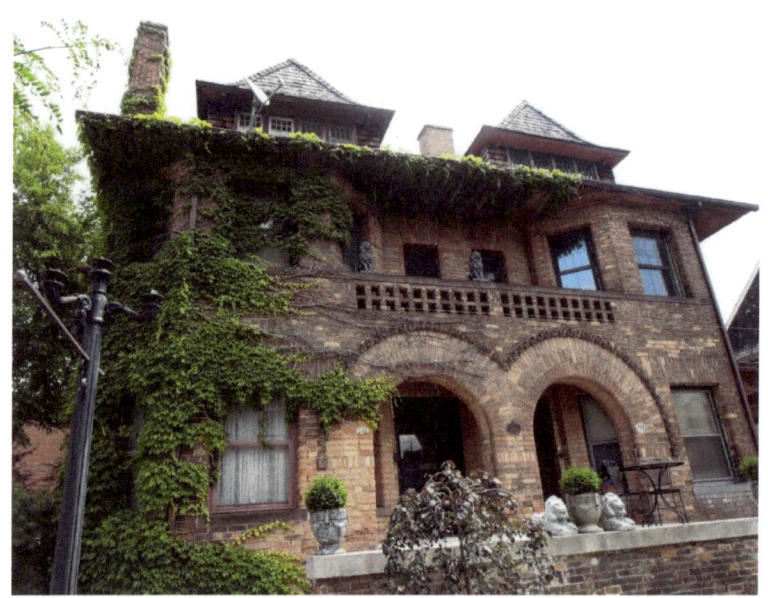

546-548 Devonshire Road built 1890 – Bed & Breakfast - 1889
Romanesque style arched entrances

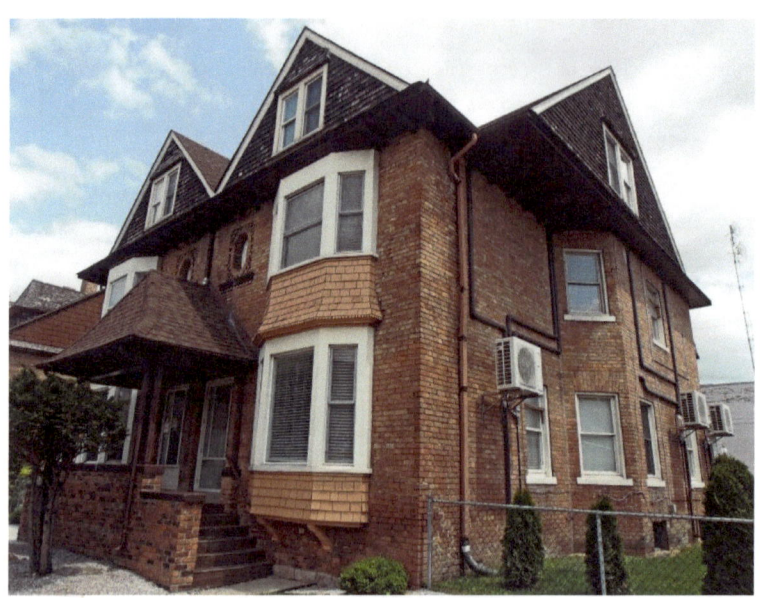

580 Devonshire Road

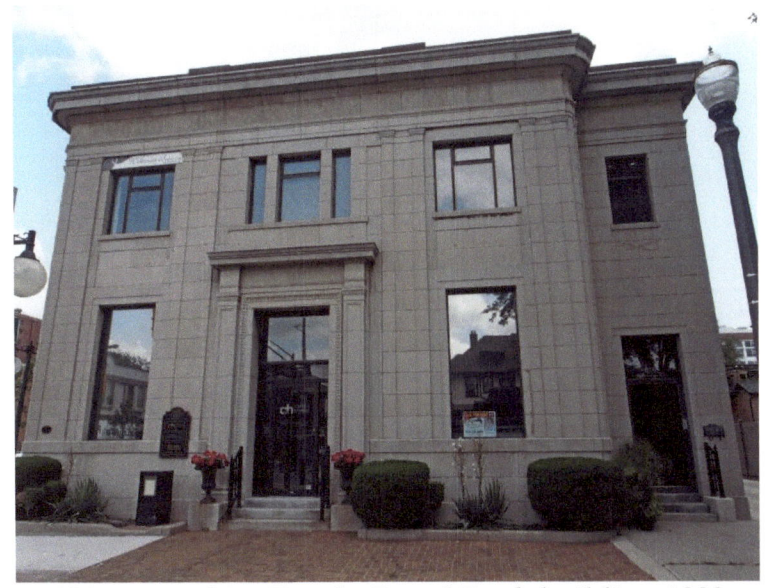

606 Devonshire Road – Royal Bank building 1922

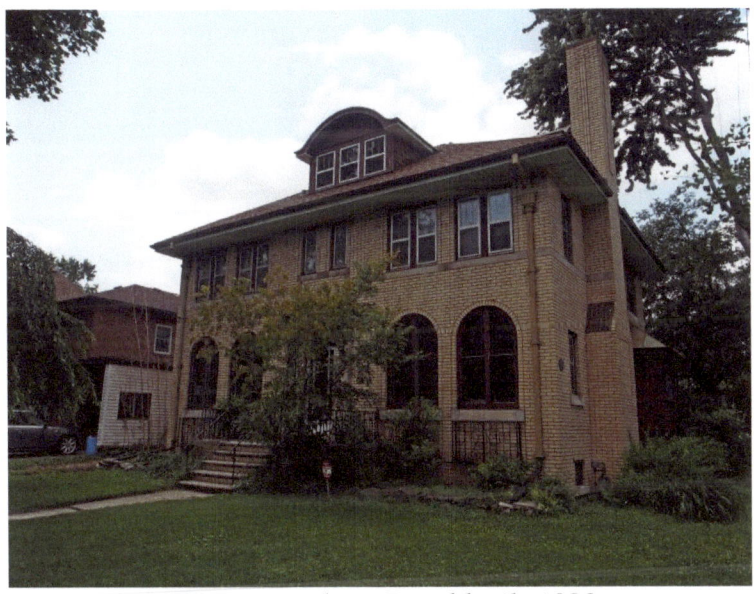

709 Devonshire Road built 1929

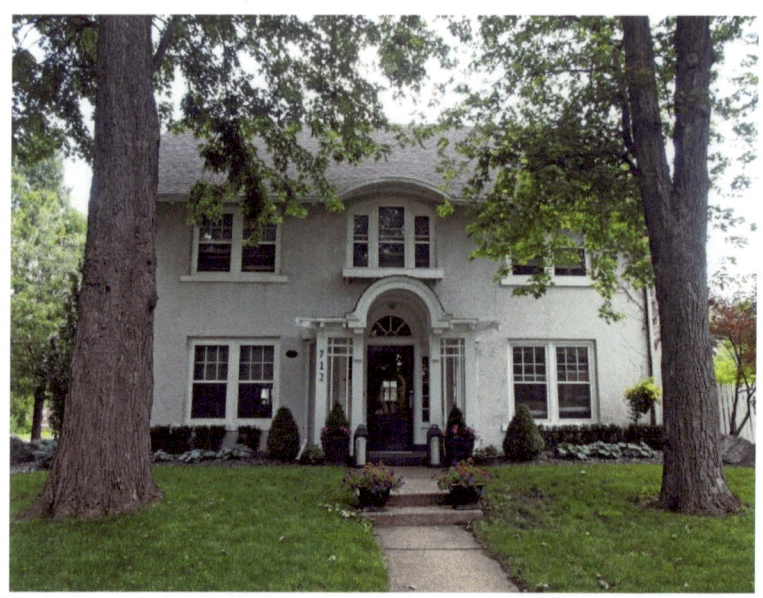

712 Devonshire Road built 1913 – The McDougall-Stodgell House – stuccoed Arts and Crafts house with wooden trellis trim in the entrance portico, in the sunroom on the south end, and in the eyebrow eaves detail which emphasizes the central window on the second floor

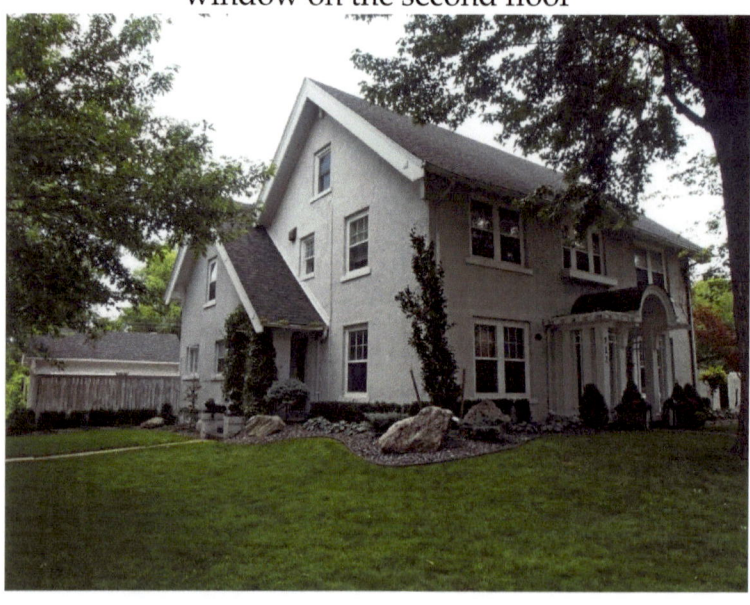

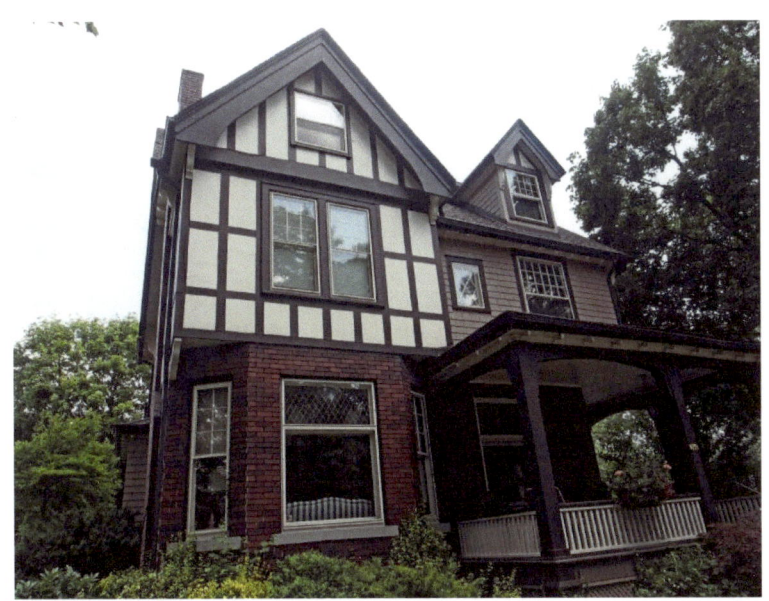

794 Devonshire Road - Porter-Coates house built 1907

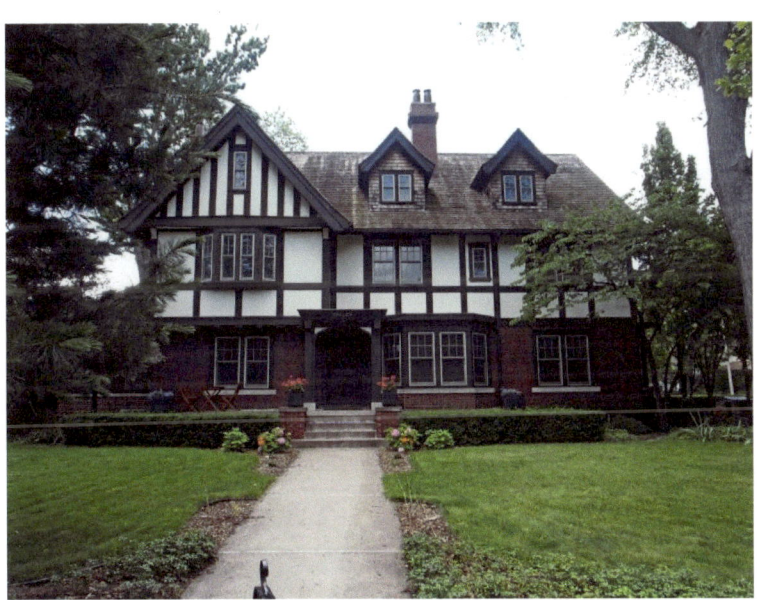

811 Devonshire Road – Foxley – The Ambery-Isaacs House – 1906-1907 Tudoresque/Arts and Crafts - half-timbered upper storey and gable, and the entrance portico blend Medieval and early 20th Century in a harmonious manner

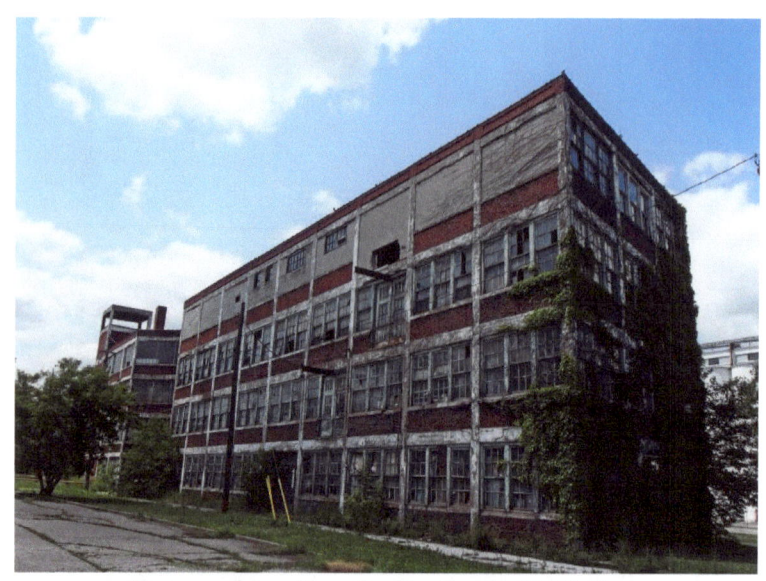

Devonshire Road - Peabody Building

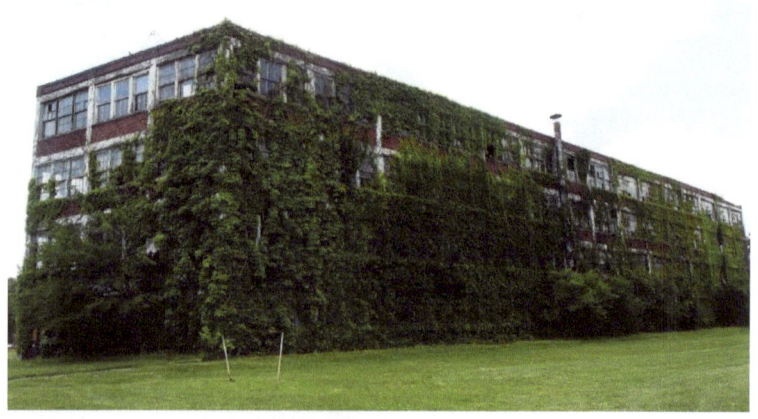

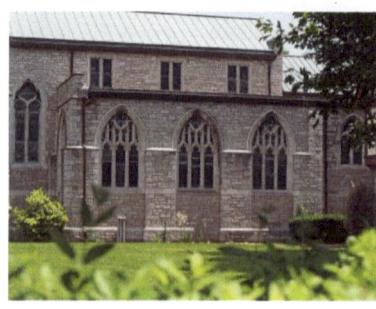

Windows St. Mary's Church

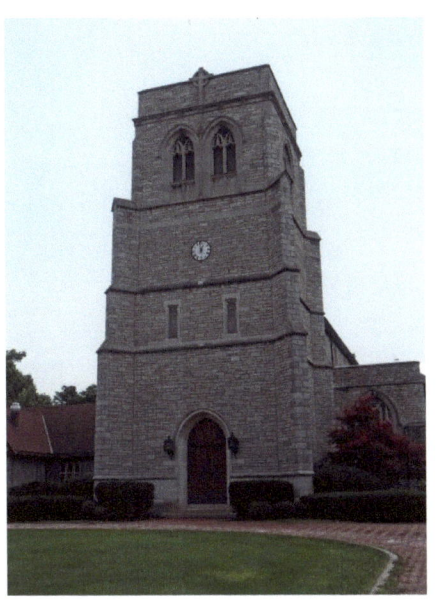

1983 St. Mary's Gate – St. Mary's Anglican Church - 1904
Gothic style

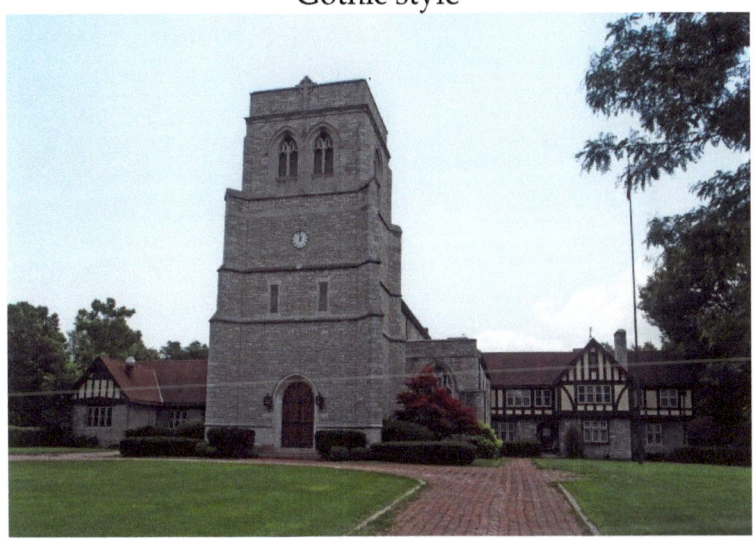

Tudor Revival Rectory and Sunday School

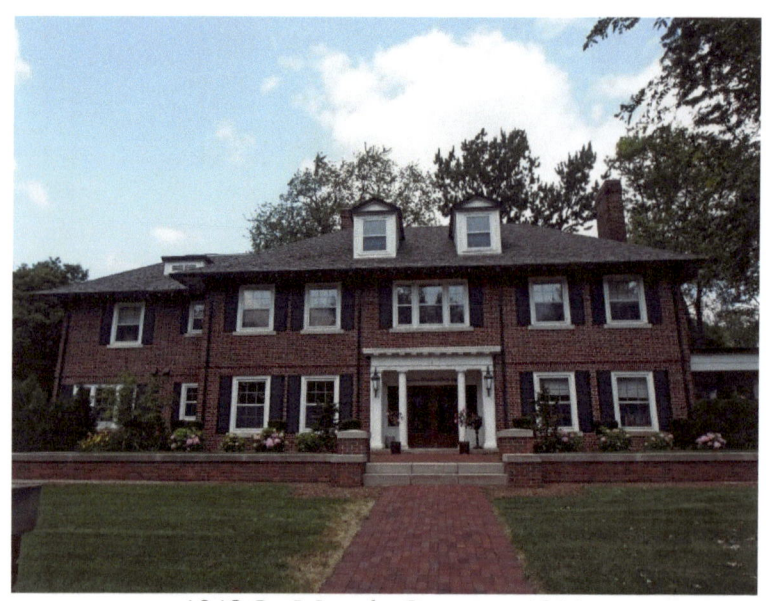

1948 St. Mary's Gate – c. 1911

End ells (an extension at the end and at right angles to the main building), dormer windows in the hipped roof, prominent entrance with a shallow entablature, sidelights

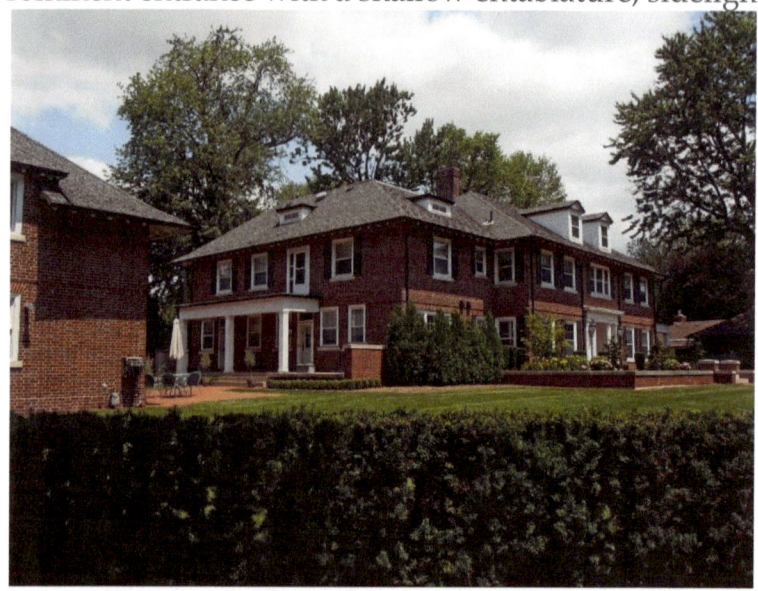

Detached garage to left of picture

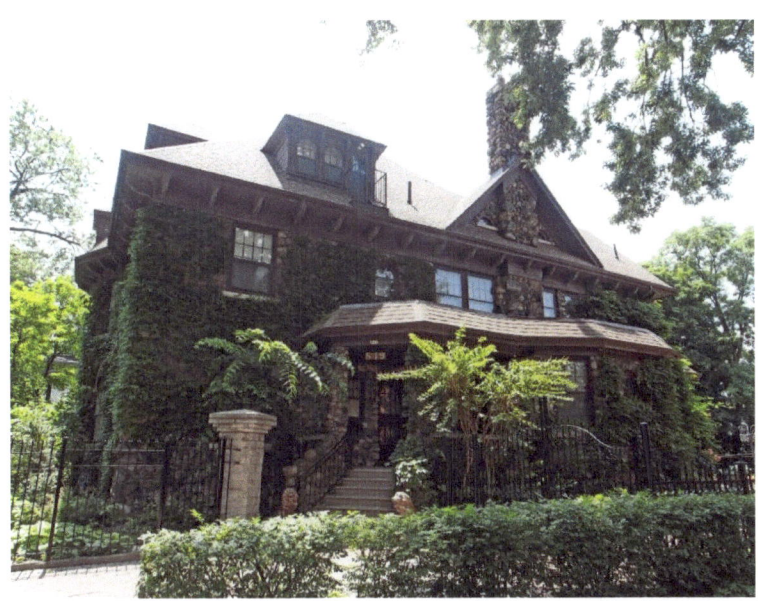

819 Kildare Road – dormer, decorative chimney

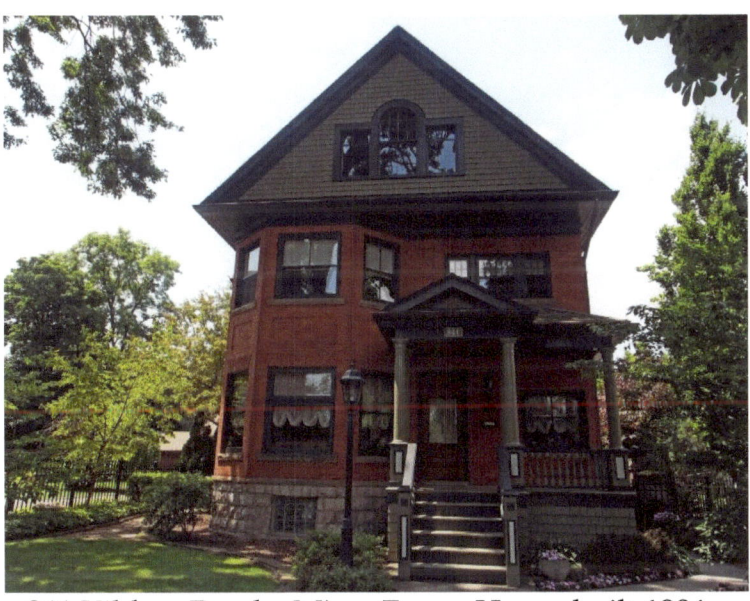

841 Kildare Road – Miers-Fraser House built 1904 –
Edwardian, Palladian window, two-storey bay, Ionic columns
supporting a pediment

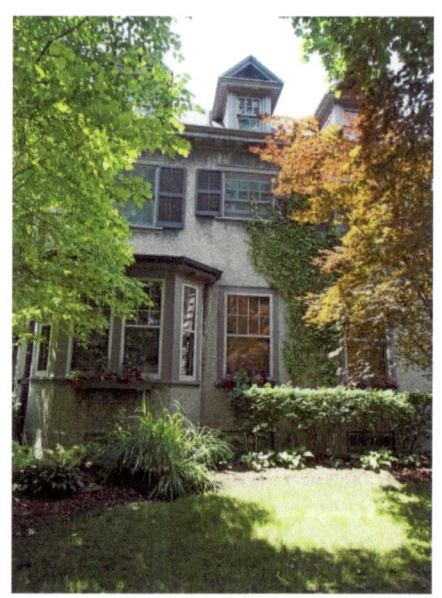

Kildare Road – dormers, bay window

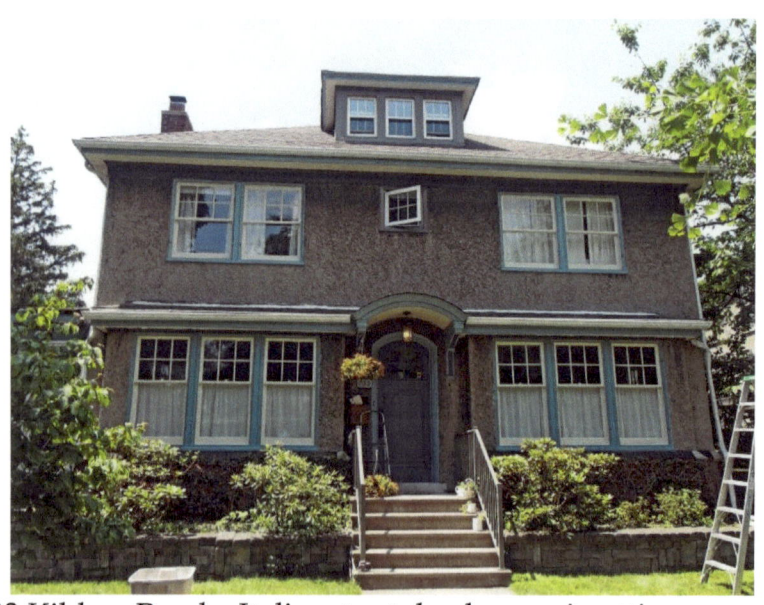

833 Kildare Road – Italianate style, dormer in attic, recessed entranceway

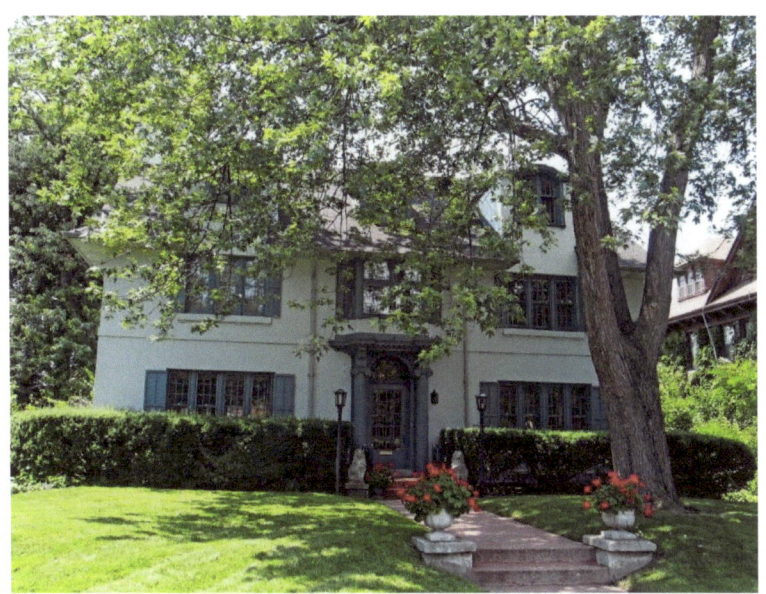

863 Kildare Road - 1908

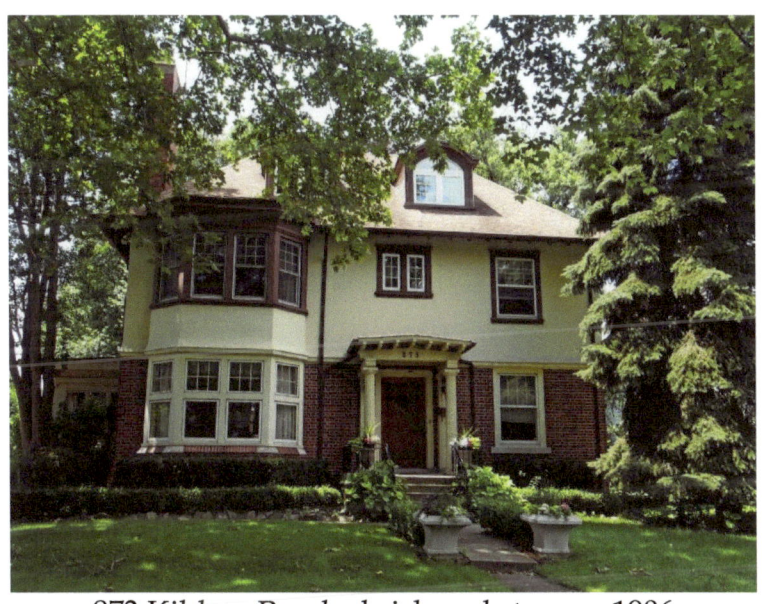

873 Kildare Road – brick and stucco - 1906

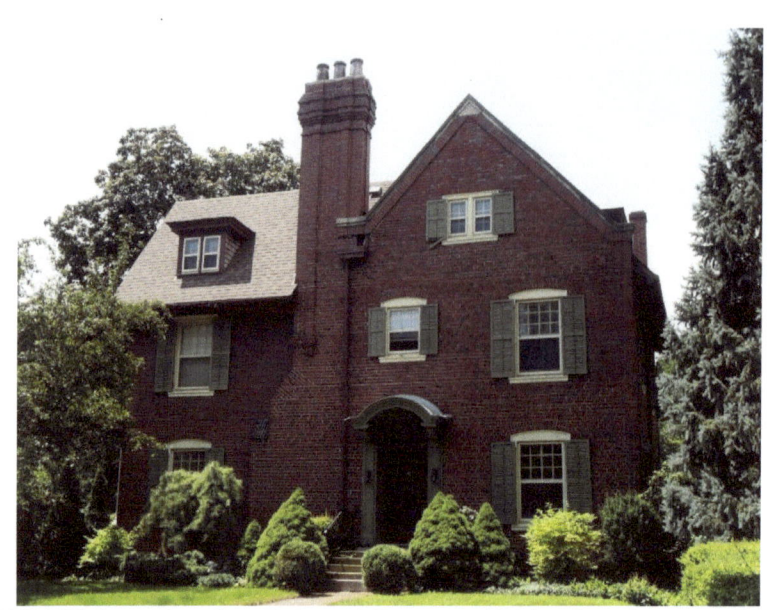

889 Kildare Road – Griggs House – 1911 – Jacobean gable,
massive ornamented chimney

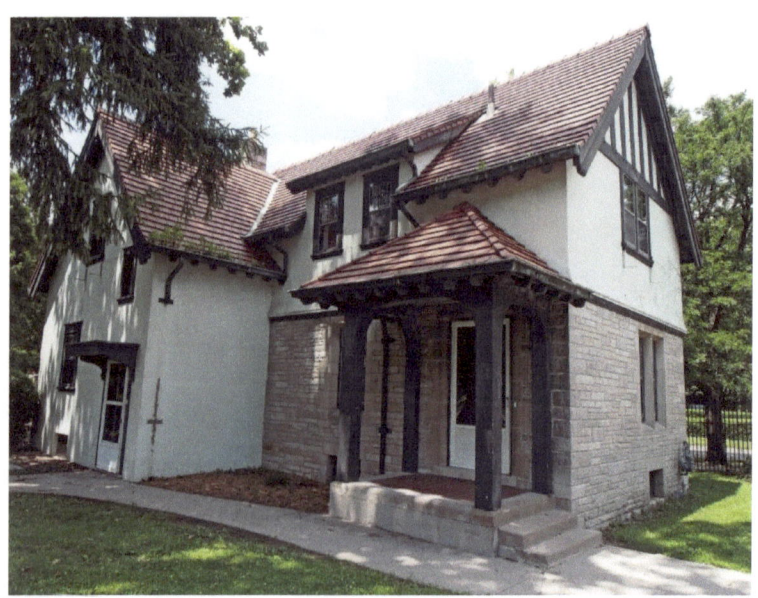

1899 Niagara Street - Willistead Manor Gate House - 1906

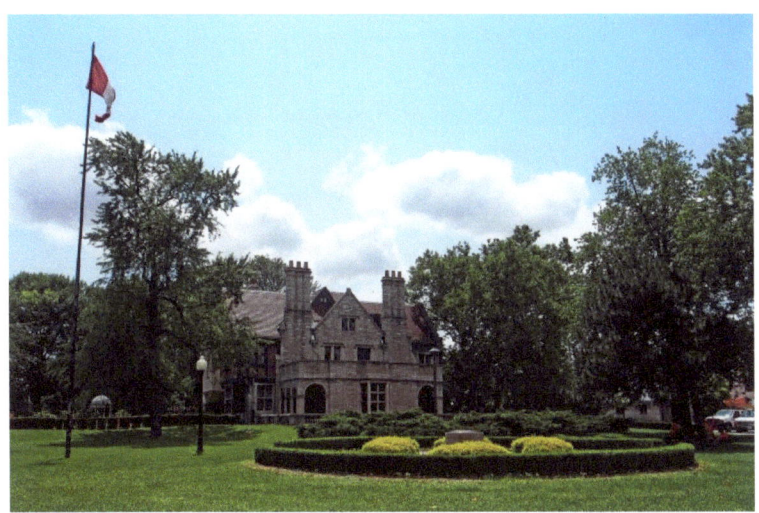

1899 Niagara Street - Willistead Manor – 1906
16th-century Tudor-Jacobean style of an English manor house was commissioned by Edward Chandler Walker, the second son of Hiram Walker.

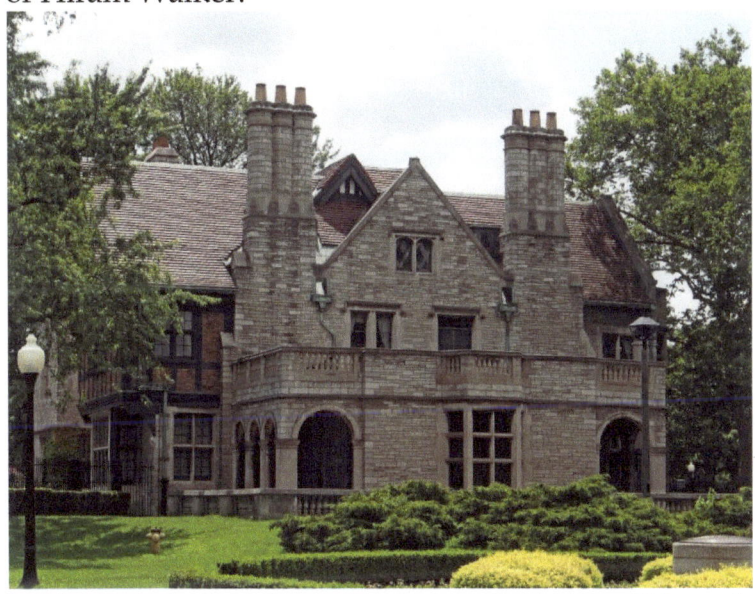

It has 36-rooms but contained only one bedroom. Edward and his wife never had any children, and the coach houses provided ample room for guests.

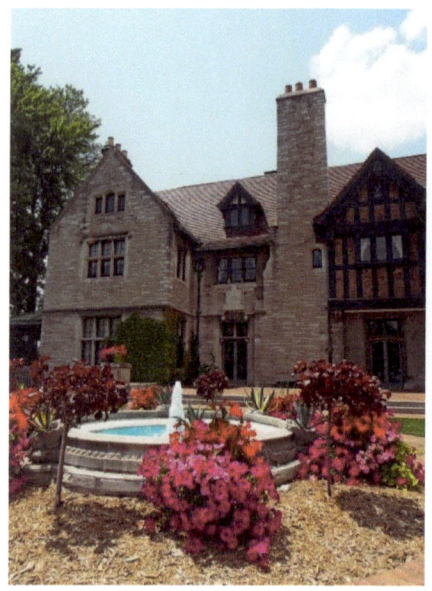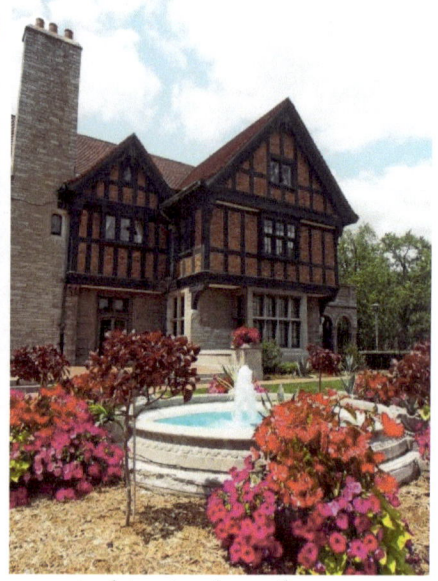

The exterior of gray limestone, quarried in Amherstburg, was hand-cut at the Willistead work site by Scottish stonemasons specifically imported for the project. Tudoresque half-timbering

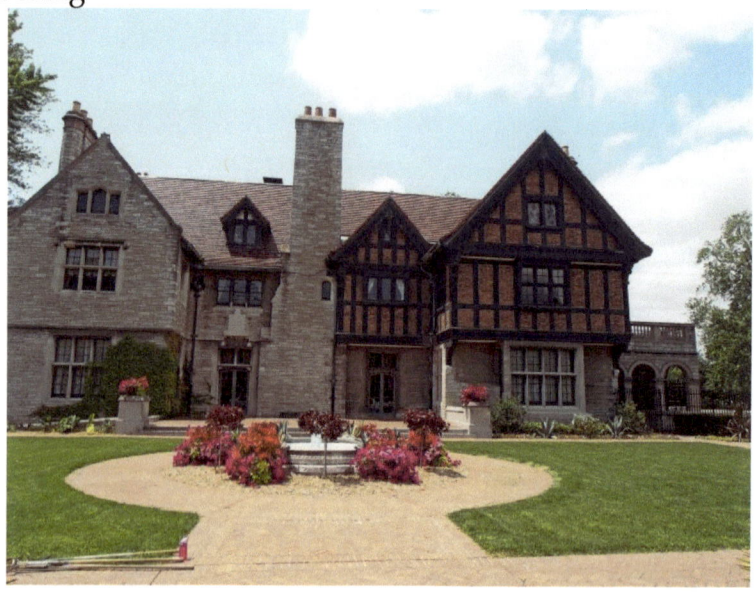

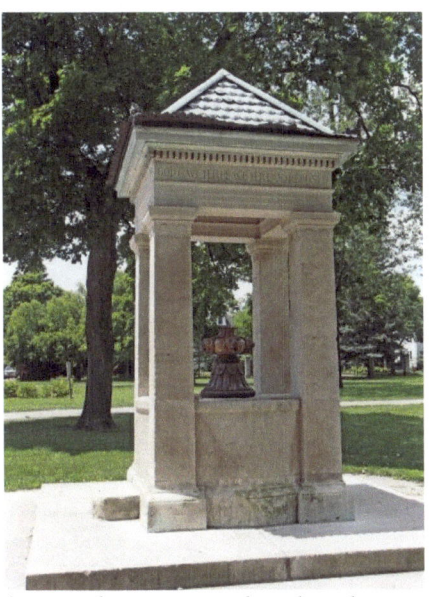

God gave her peace, her land reposed
Her court was pure, her life serene
A thousand claims to reverence closed
In her as wife, mother, and queen.

To commemorate the completion of the 60th year of the
glorious reign of her most gracious majesty Queen Victoria

This gift of Hiram Walker & Sons Limited to the people of
Walkerville MDCCCXCVII 1897

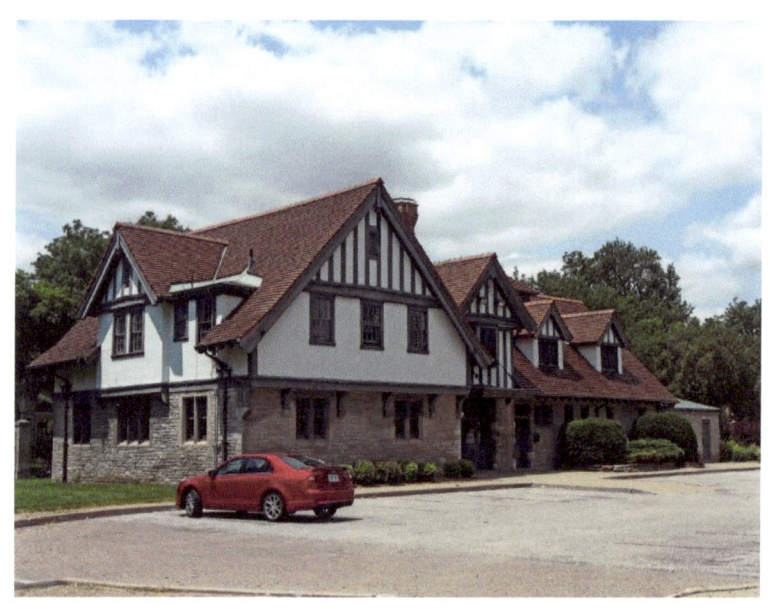

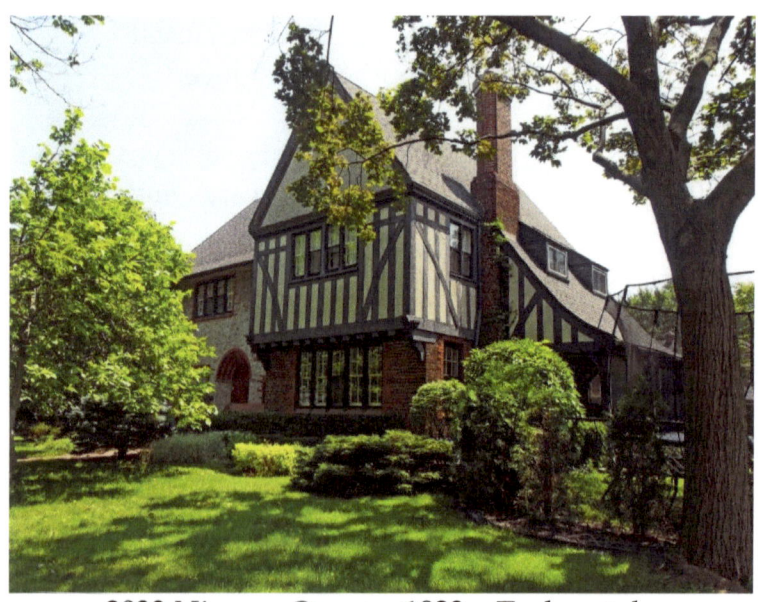

2033 Niagara Street – 1923 – Tudor style

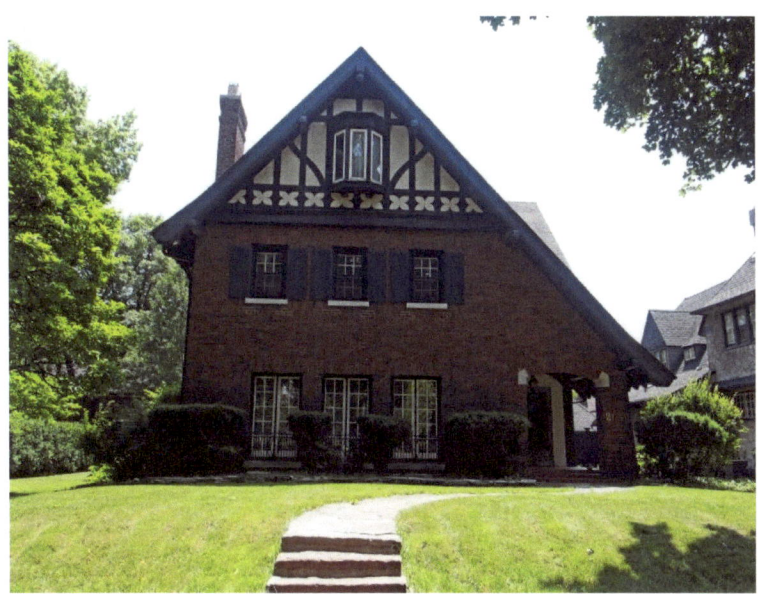

2049 Niagara Street – 1922 – olive green mortar used
Tudor half-timbering

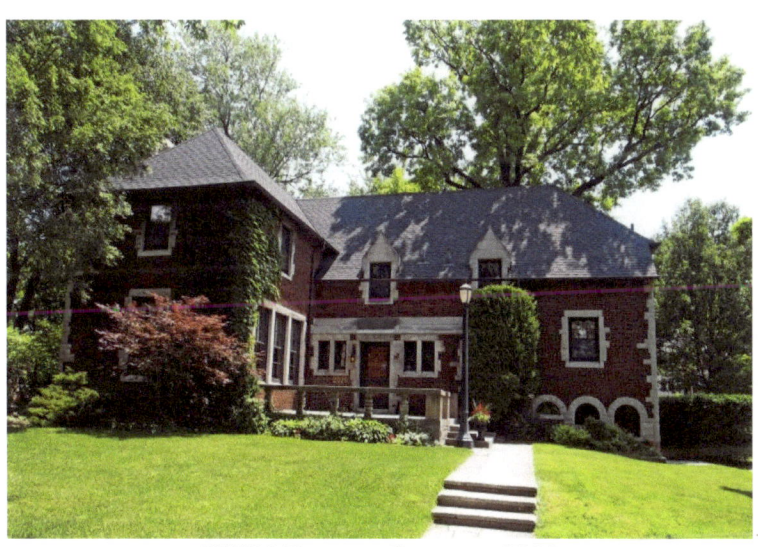

2079 Niagara Street – 1929

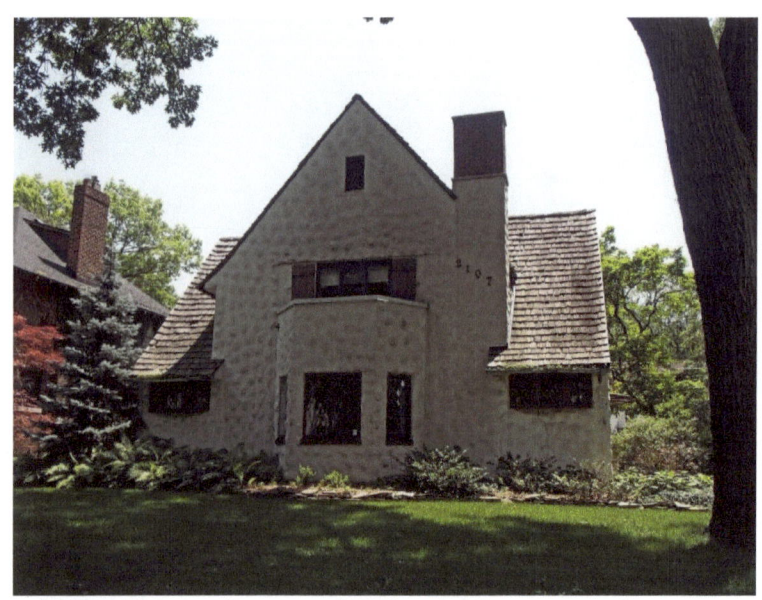

2107 Niagara Street – 1925 – richly textured stucco,
Jacobean gable

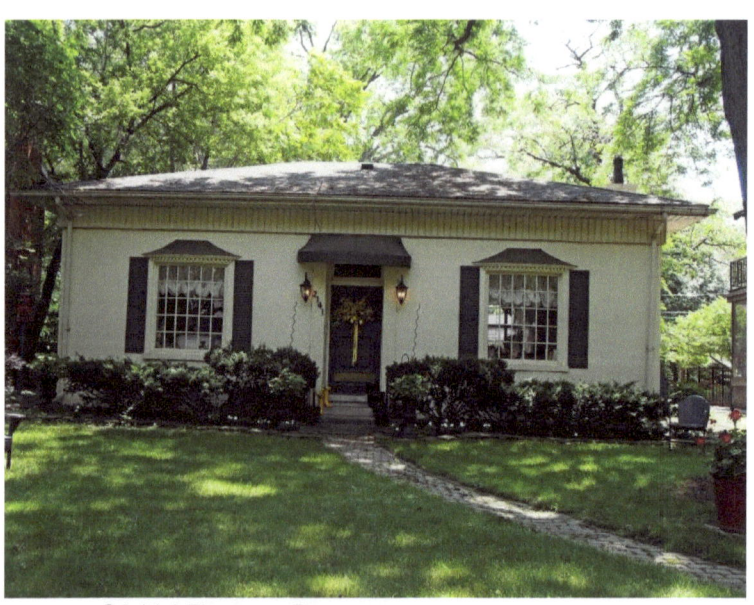

2141 Niagara Street – one storey cottage

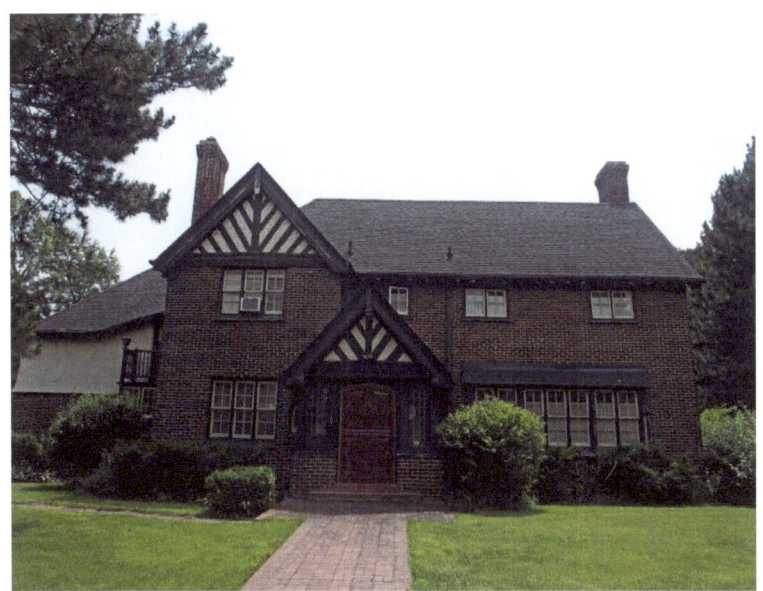

1941 Richmond Street – Tudor half-timbering

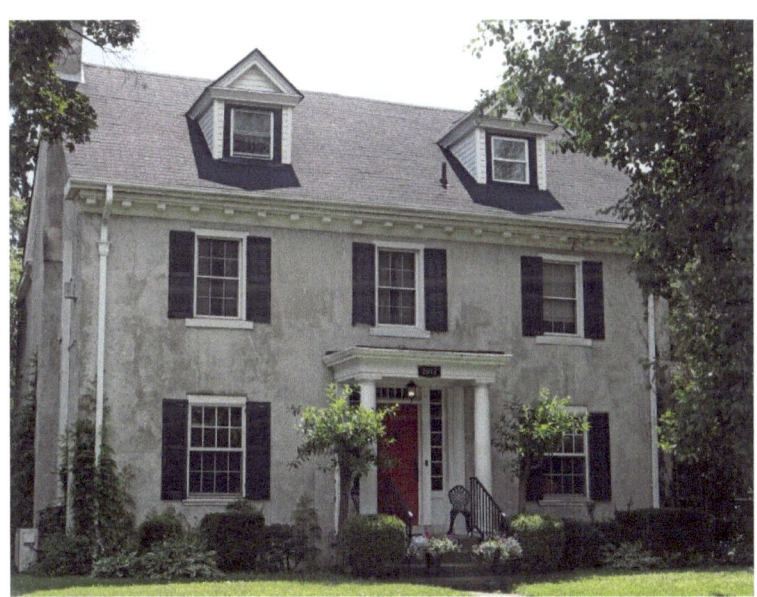

2017 Richmond Street – two-storey Georgian style stucco building, dormers, pillared entranceway, sidelights and transom window

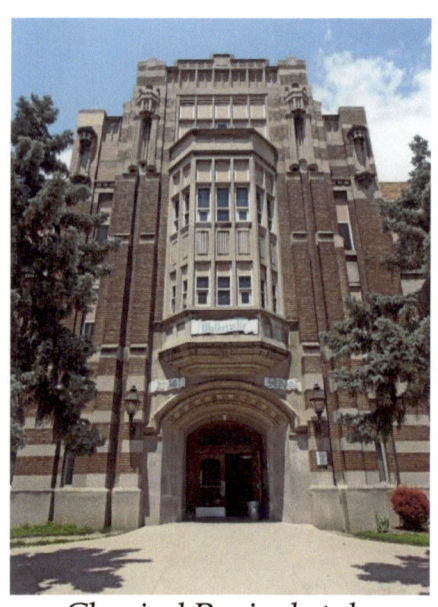

Classical Revival style

2100 Richmond Street - Walkerville Collegeiate - 1922

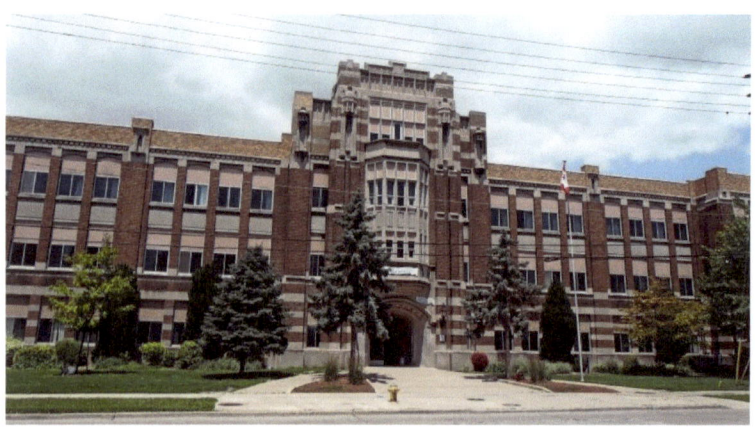

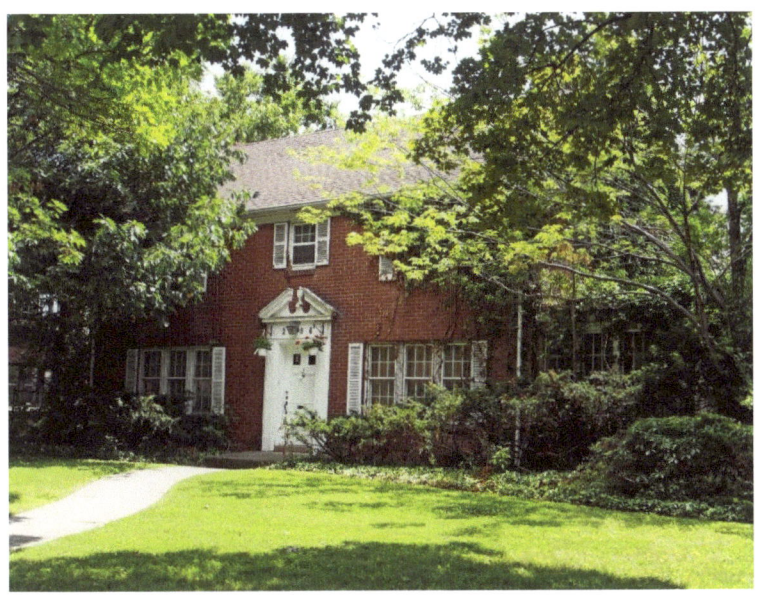

Willistead Crescent – burst pediment above door

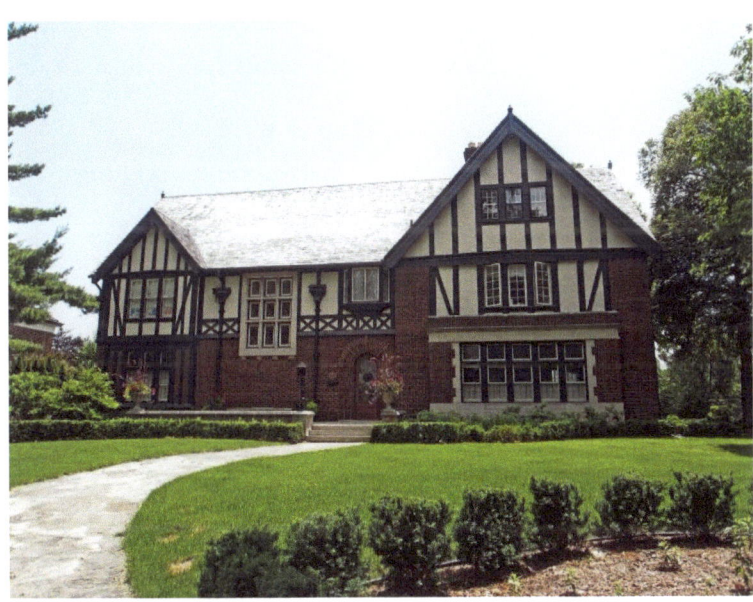

2088 Willistead Crescent – Tudor style
Dr. Charles W. Hoare Residence - 1920

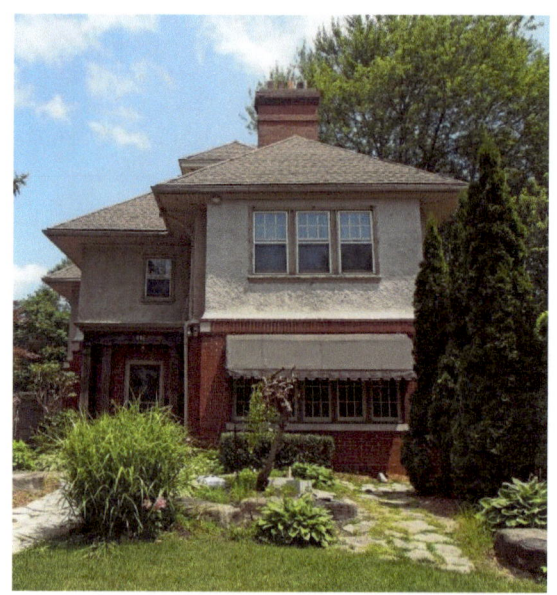

982 Willistead Crescent

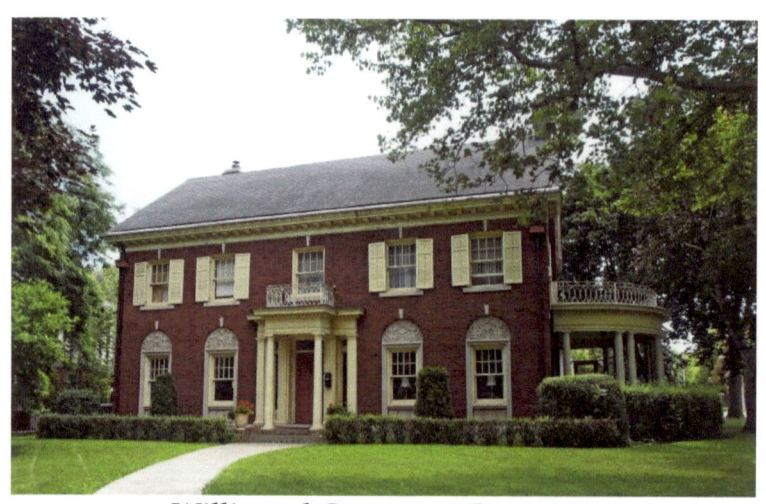

Willistead Crescent - Georgian

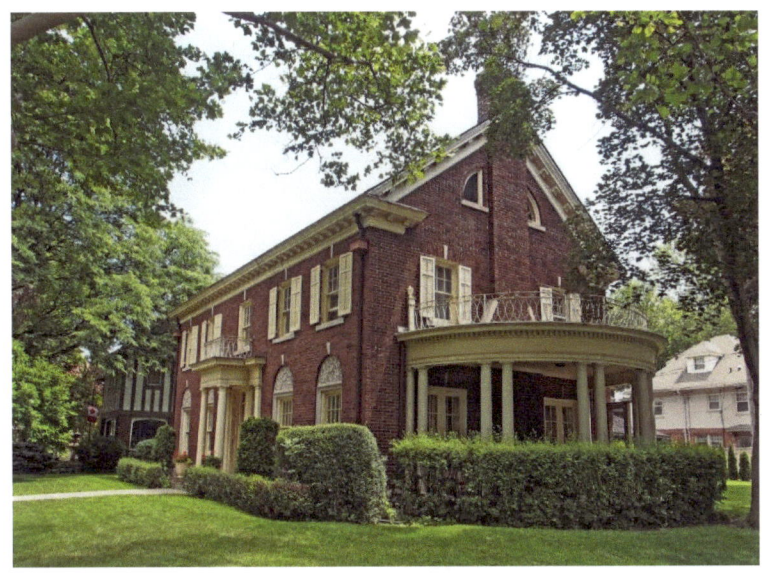

Willistead Crescent

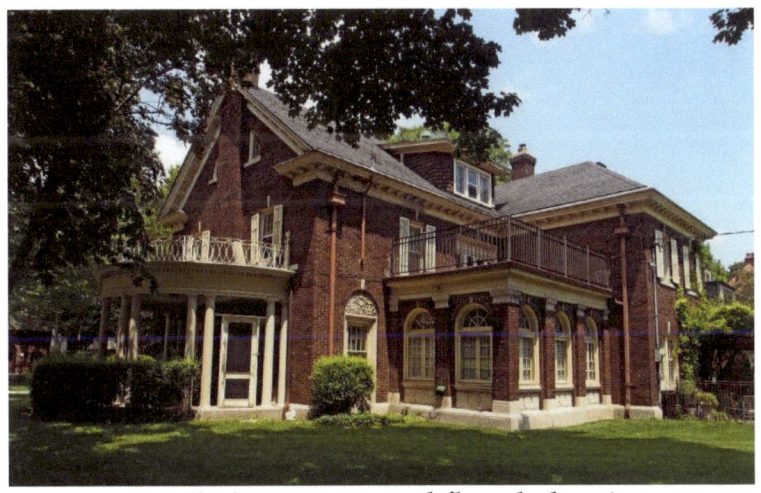

Dentilled eaves, second floor balconies,
cornice return on end gable, dormer in attic

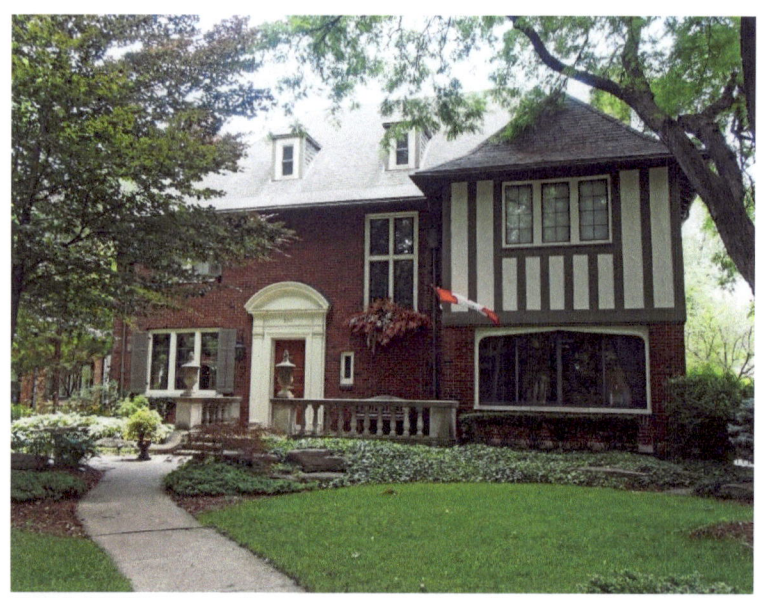

2011 Willistead Crescent – G. Tate Easton House 1926
Arts and Crafts house with Tudoresque half-timbering

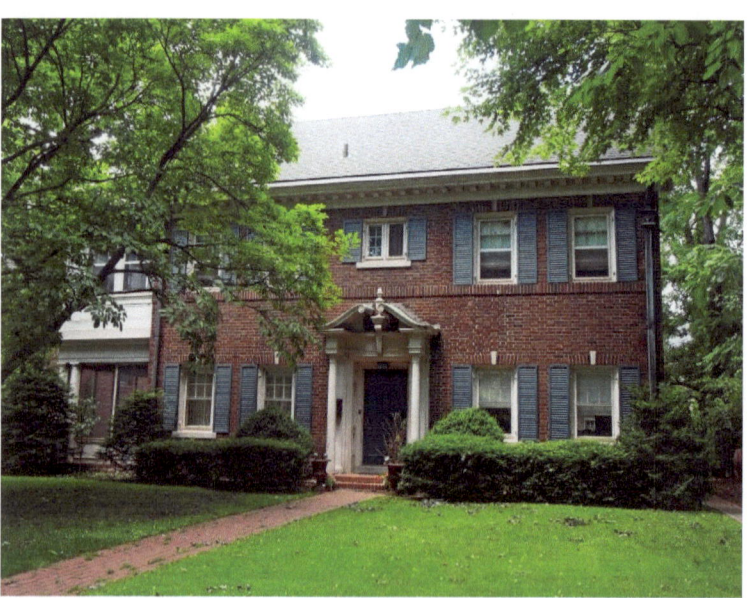

2008 Willistead Crescent – Georgian – burst pediment above
columned entranceway

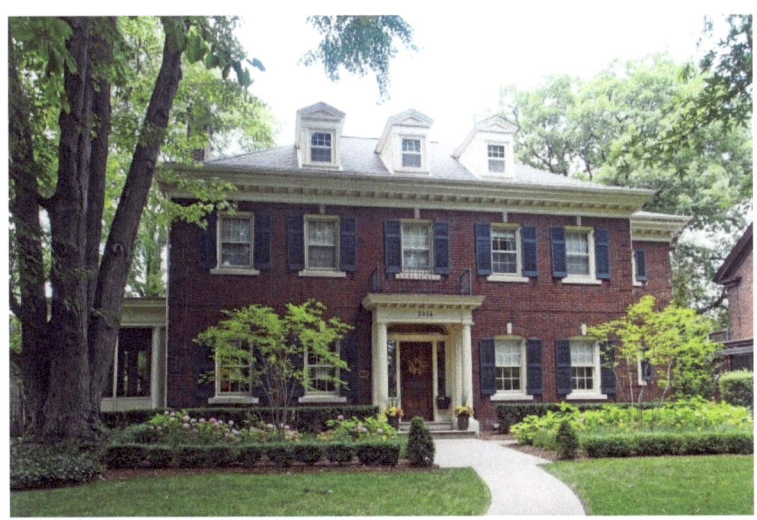

2014 Willistead Crescent – Dr. Henry Crassweller House –
1925 - Colonial Revival style

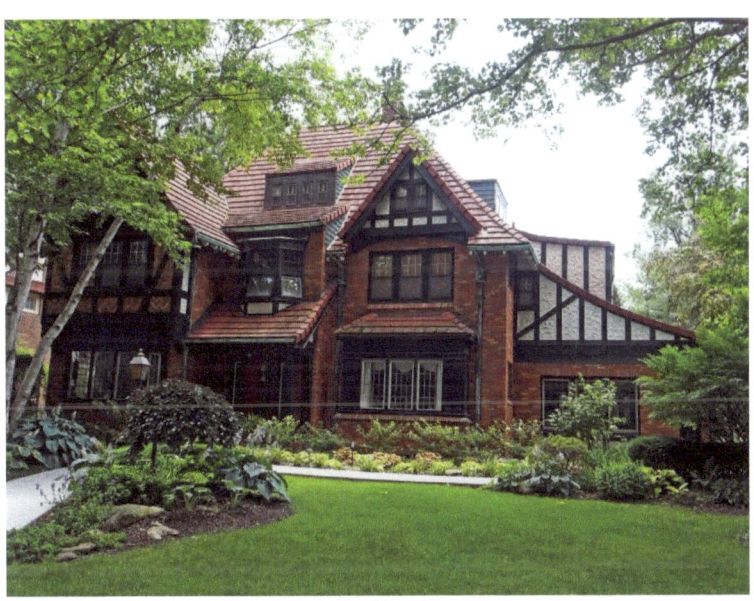

2019 Willistead Crescent – Tudoresque Arts and Crafts

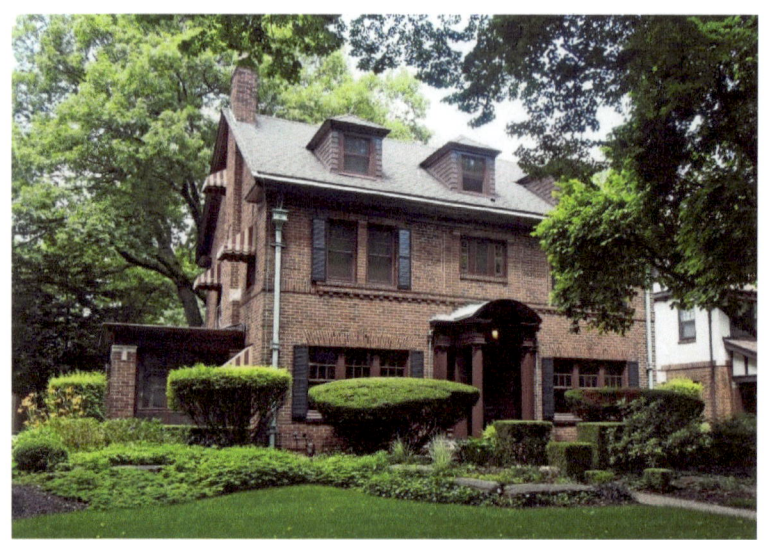

2020 Willistead Crescent – 1925 – Georgian, dentils, dormers

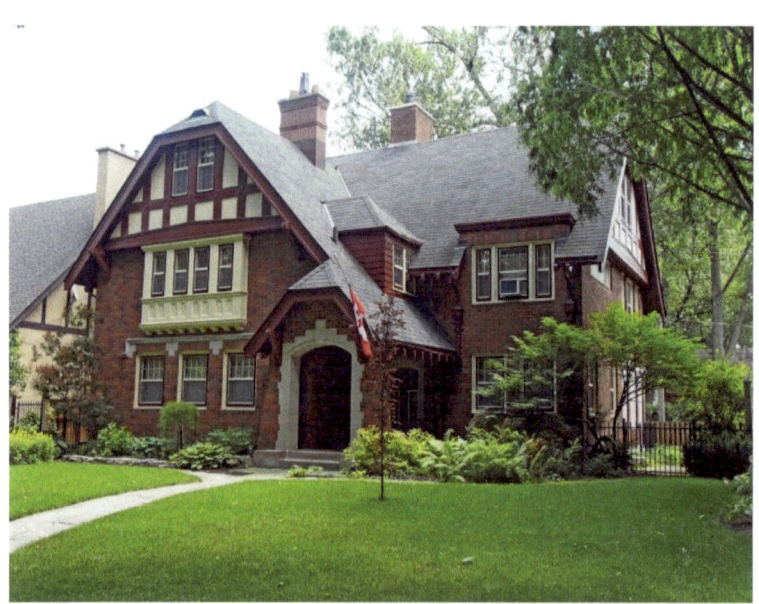

2025 Willistead Crescent – 1929 – Tudoresque Arts and Crafts

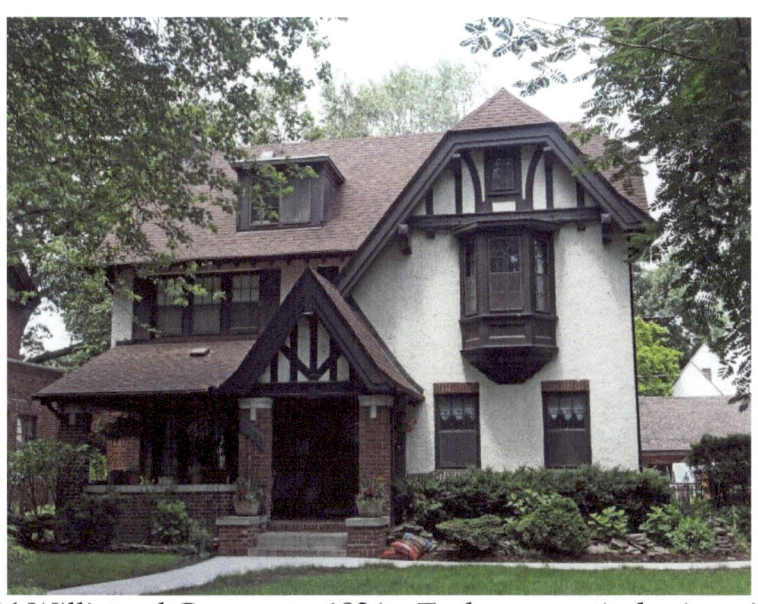

2026 Willistead Crescent – 1924 – Tudoresque timbering, Arts and Crafts stucco, oriel window

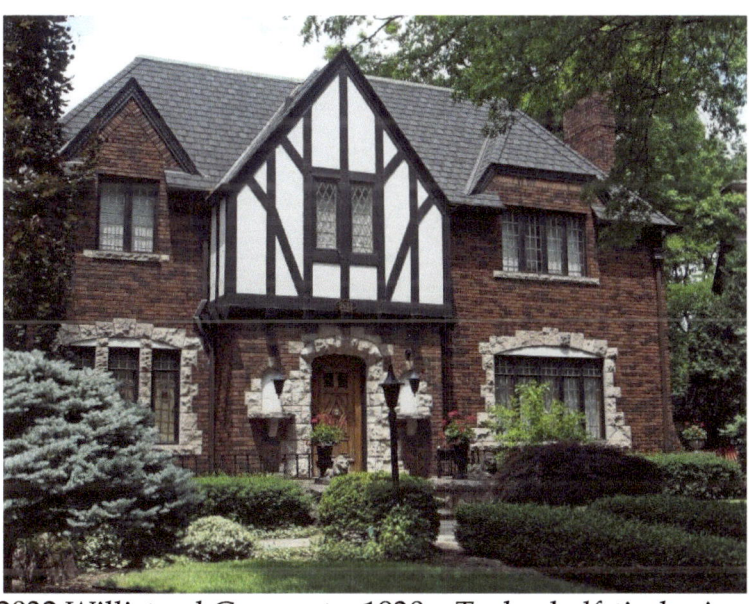

2032 Willistead Crescent – 1930 – Tudor half-timbering, Arts and Crafts

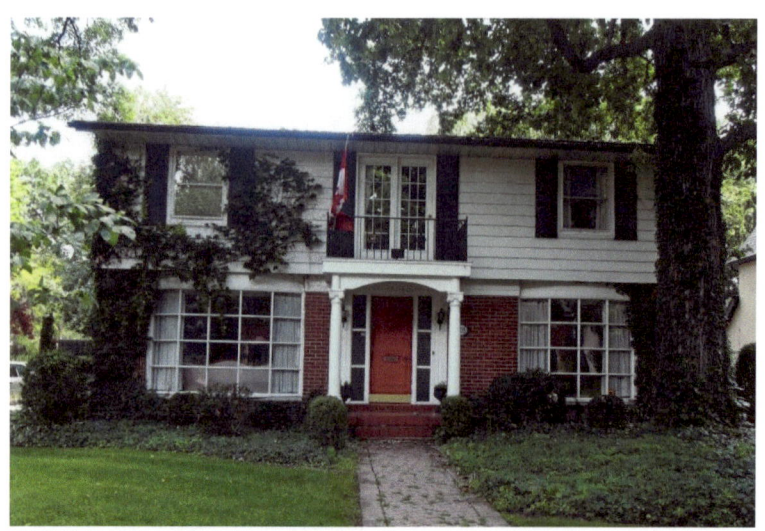

2035 Willistead Crescent – Georgian, Ionic capitals on columned porch supports with balcony above

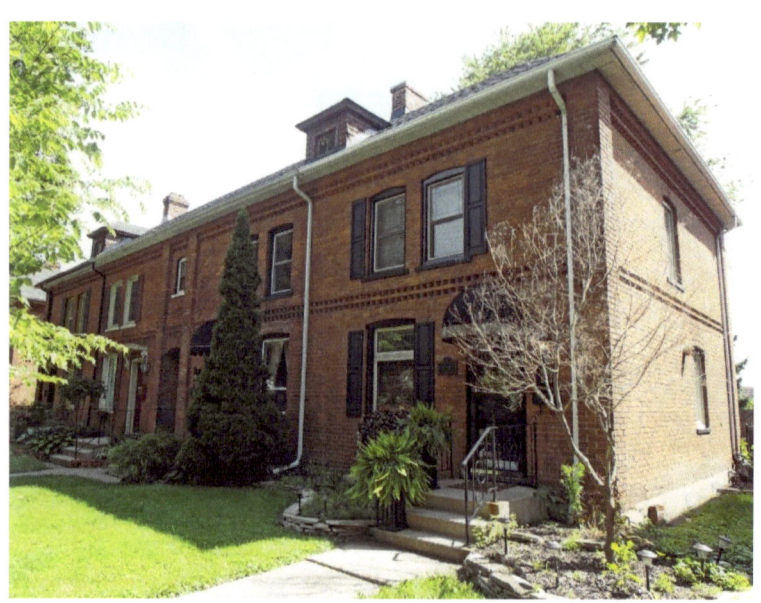

Monmouth Road

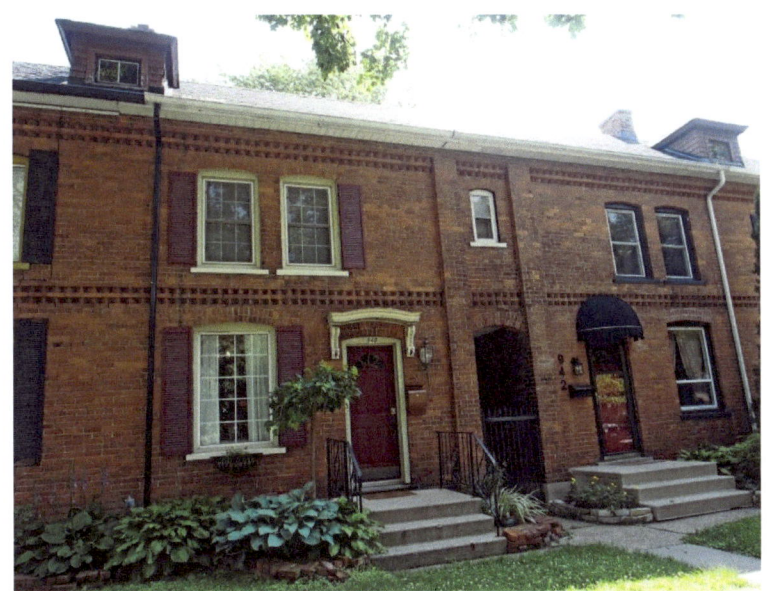

940-942 Monmouth Road – dormers, dentil brickwork

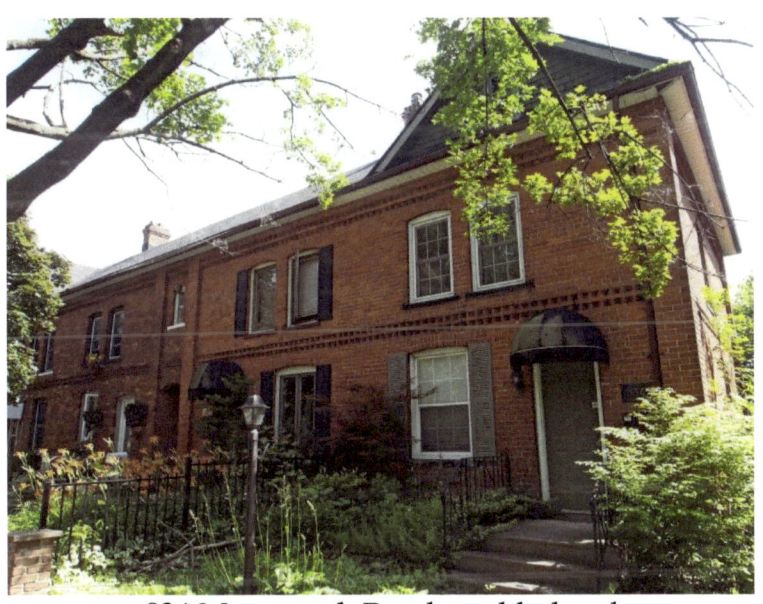

934 Monmouth Road – gabled end

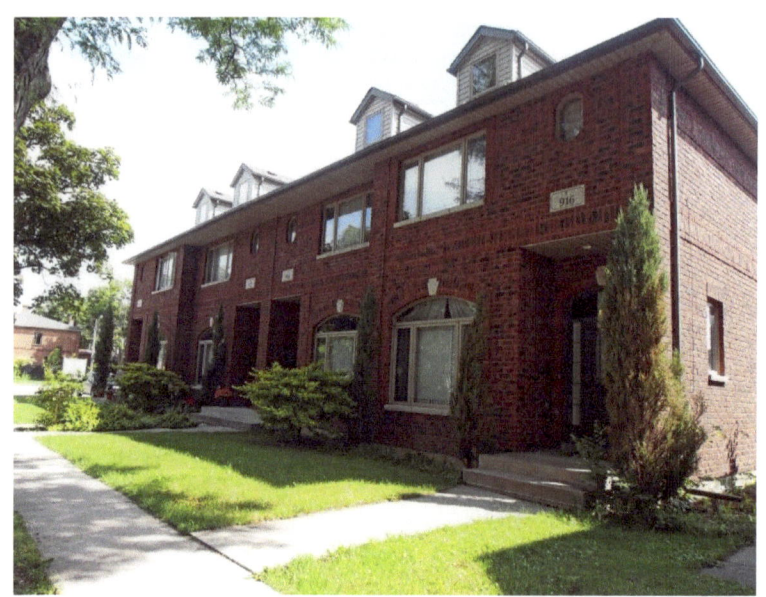

910-916 Monmouth Road

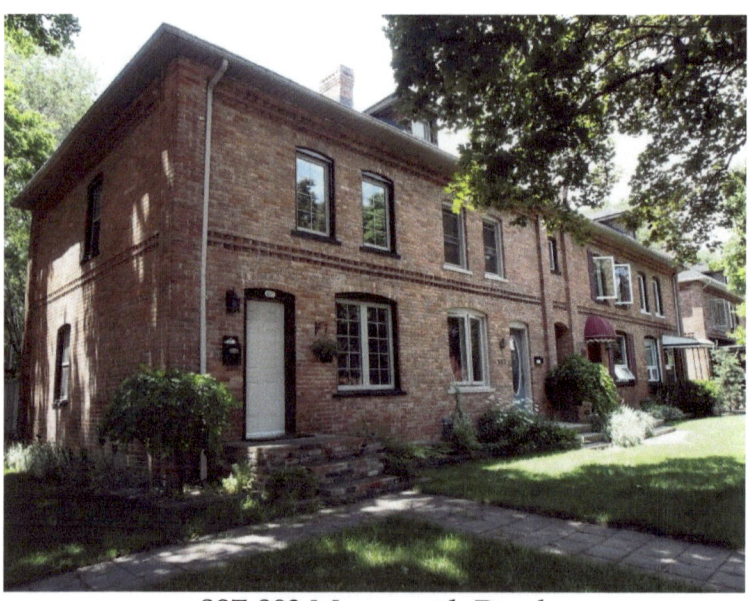

897-893 Monmouth Road

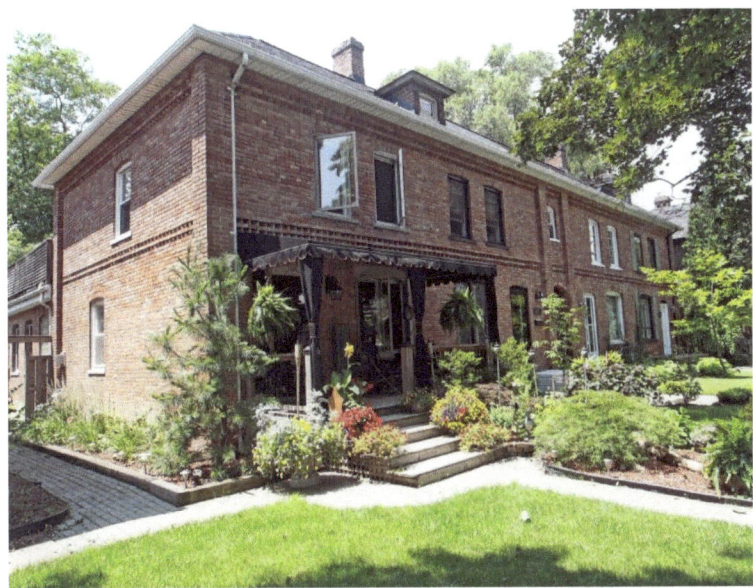
883-879 Monmouth Road

Both sides of Monmouth Road are lined with dark red brick houses for the workers at the distillery and other industries in Walkerville. The 800 block has twelve row houses with four units each. At the middle of the block are two semi-detached houses intended for the foremen and their families.

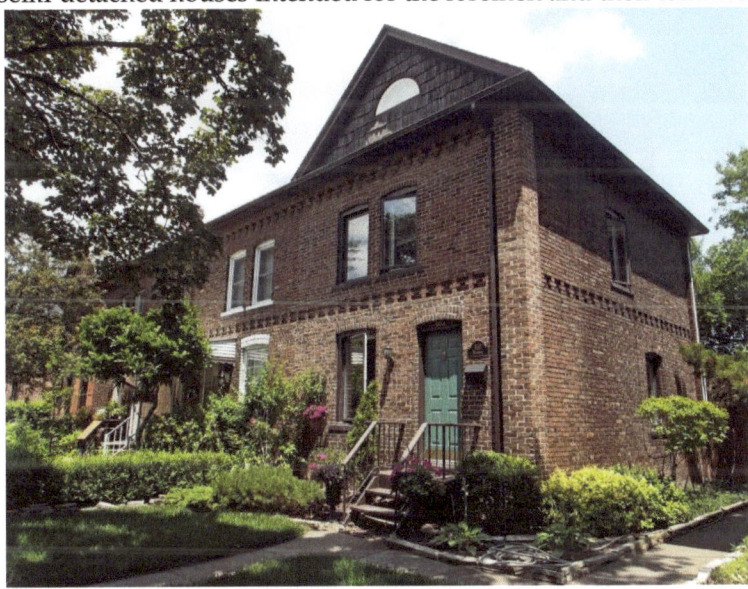
868-864 Monmouth Road – dentil brickwork

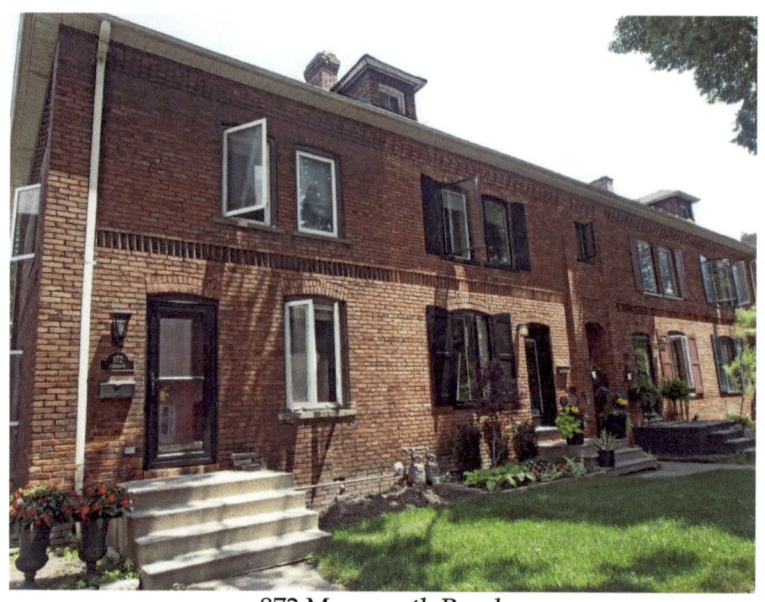
872 Monmouth Road

There is a great variety of detail in the residences. Some have flat parapets, some have end gables, and others have paired frontal gables. All terraces have central open passageways leading to the rear yards. A variety of decorative brickwork is evident, giving interesting texture to the houses and to the streetscape.

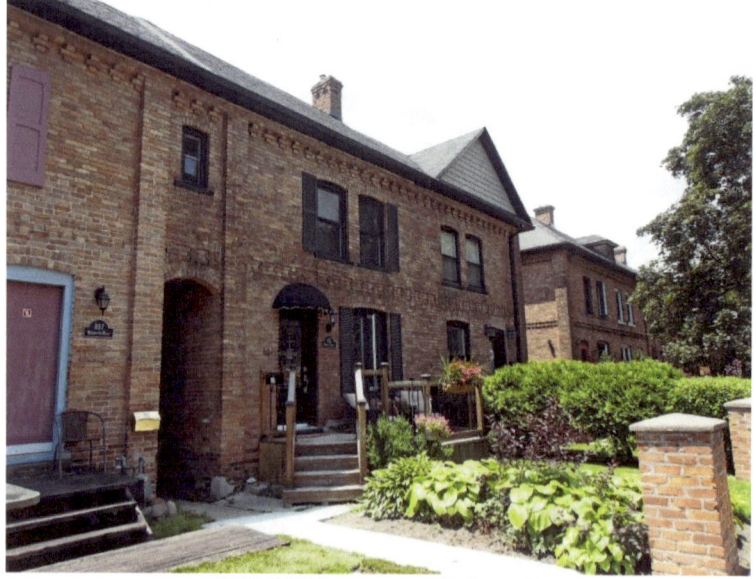
837-835 Monmouth Road

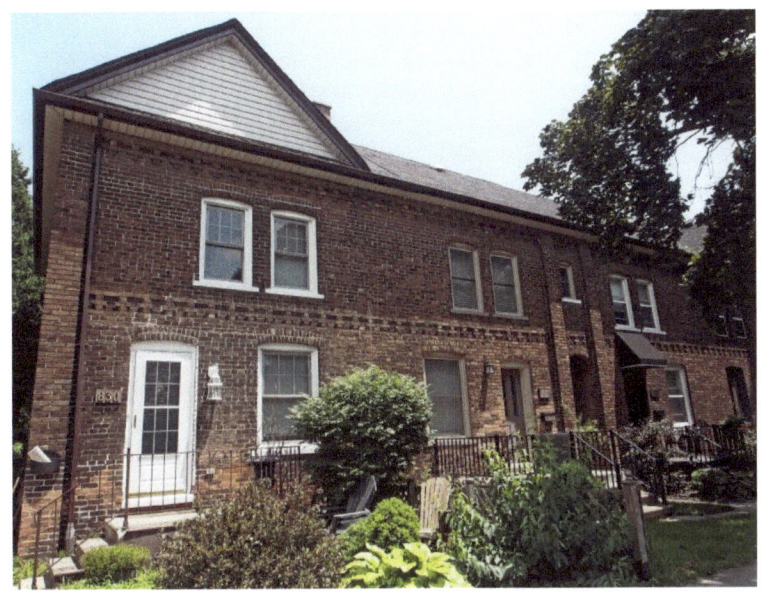

830-834 Monmouth Road – decorative brickwork

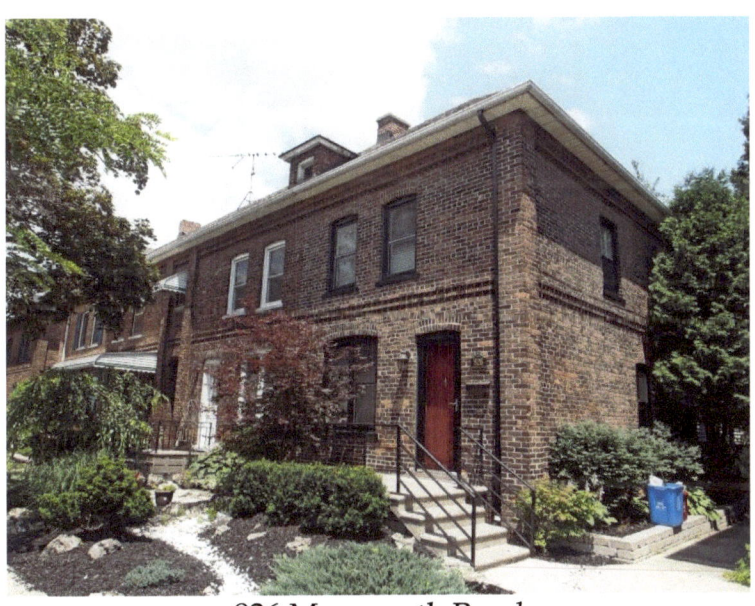

826 Monmouth Road

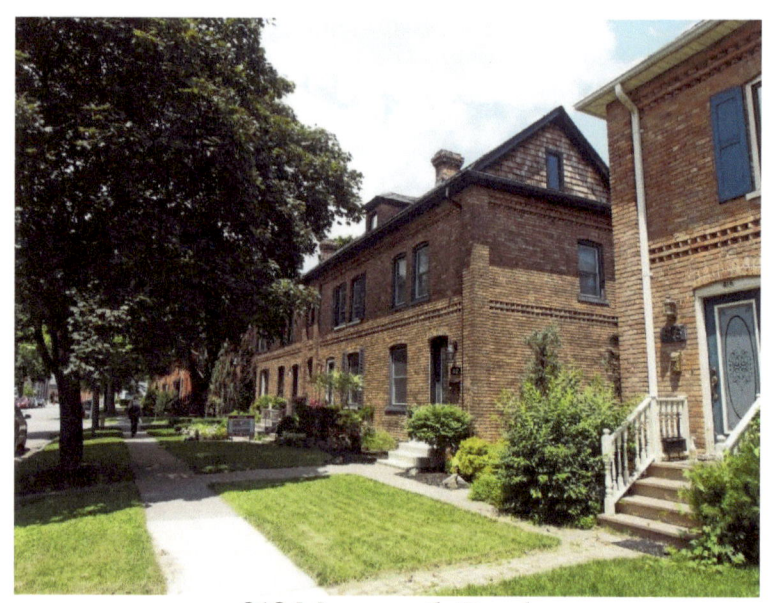

812 Monmouth Road

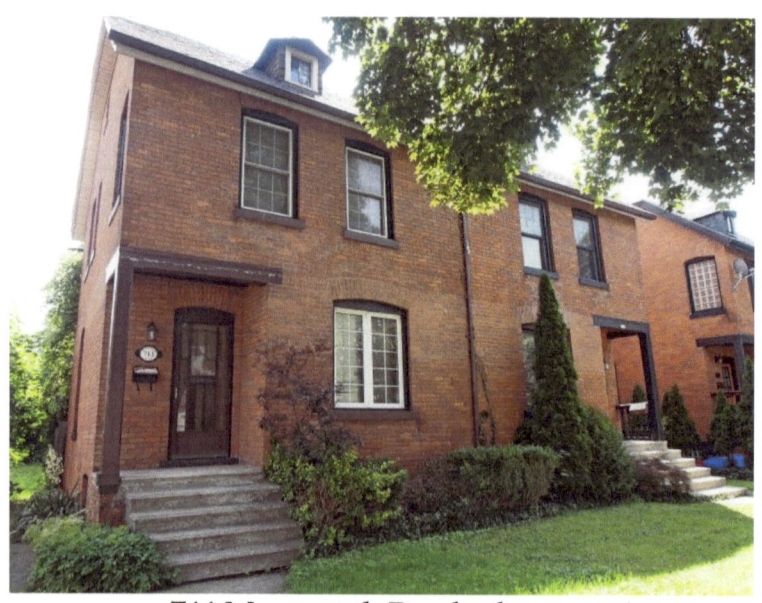

744 Monmouth Road - dormer

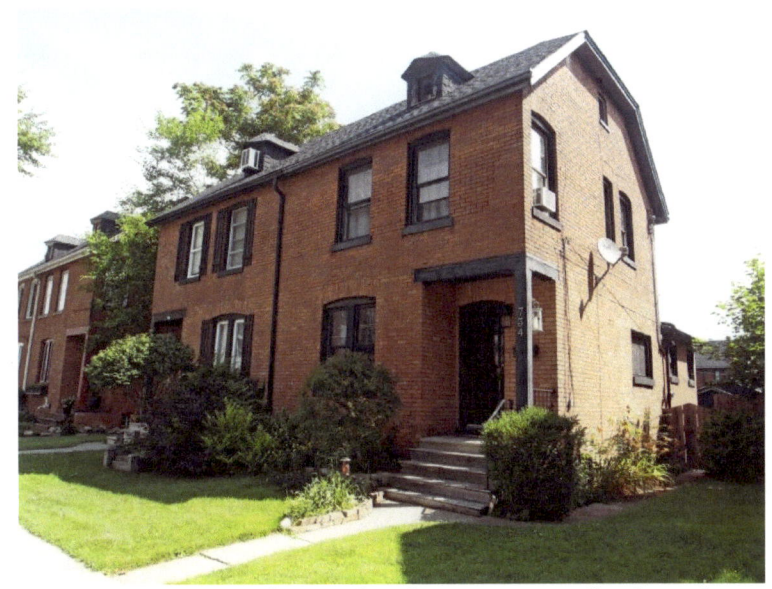

734 Monmouth Road – dormers, gambrel roof

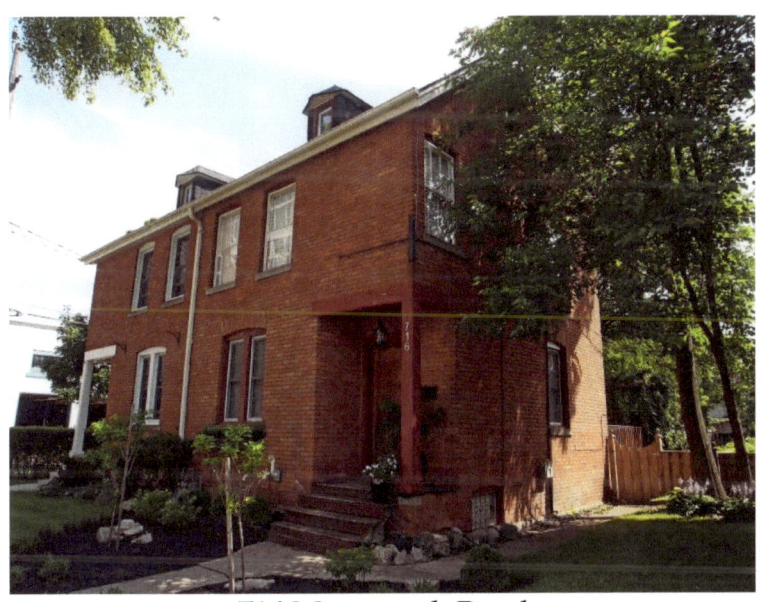

716 Monmouth Road

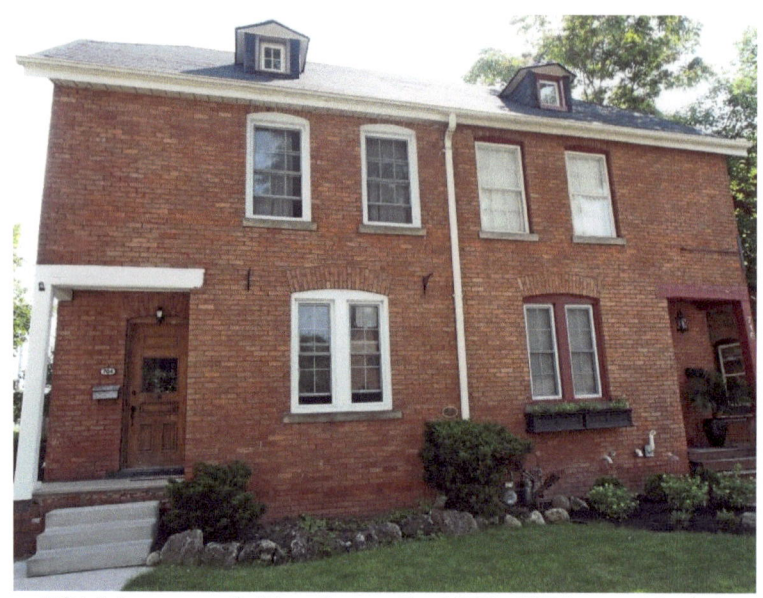

704 Monmouth Road – early 1893-1894 – red brick
semi-detached, dormers

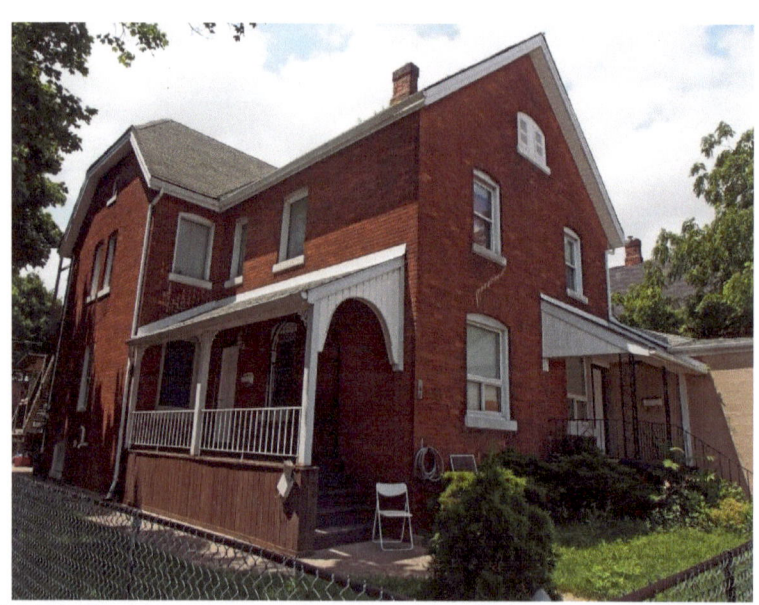

785 Walker Road – gambrel roof on far end, gabled roof on
near end

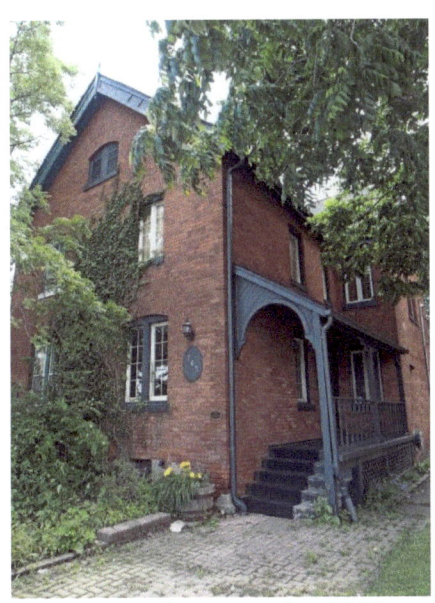

763 Walker Road – 1893

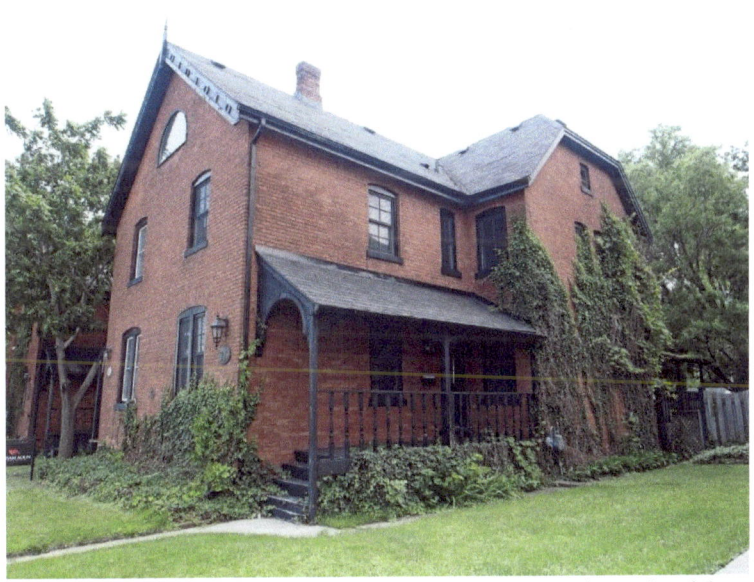

749 Walker Road – one of five identical semi-detached houses
on the west side of Walker Road

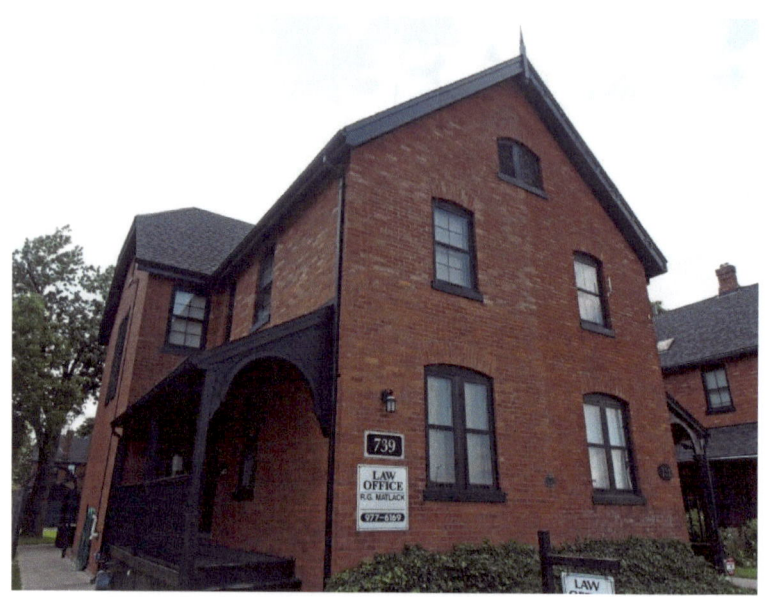

739 Walker Road

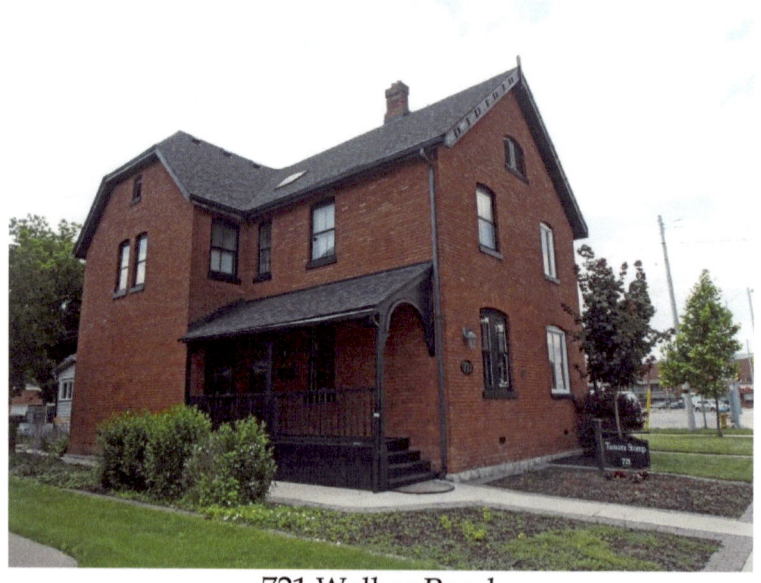

721 Walker Road

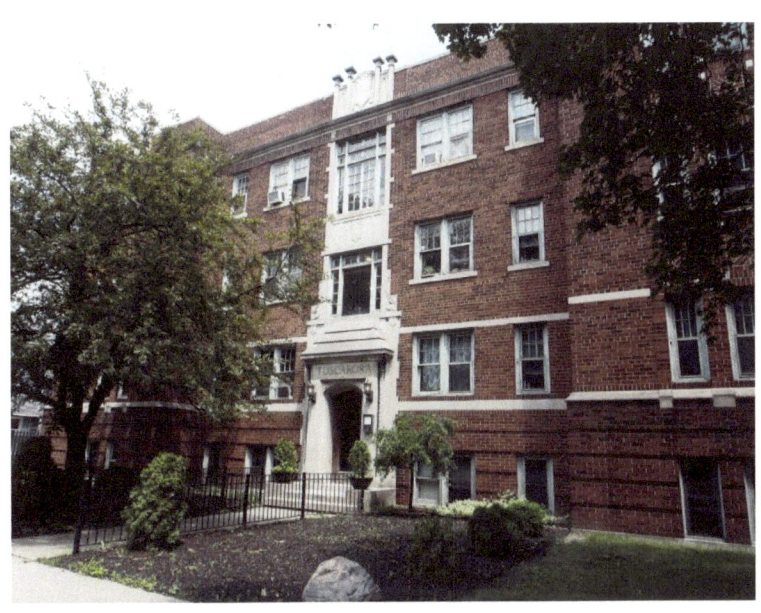

The Tuscarora Apartment Block
686 Argyle Road – Classical Revival style

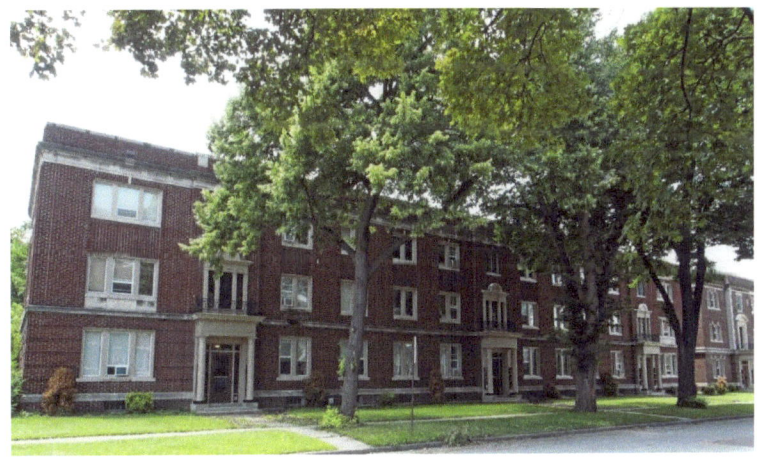

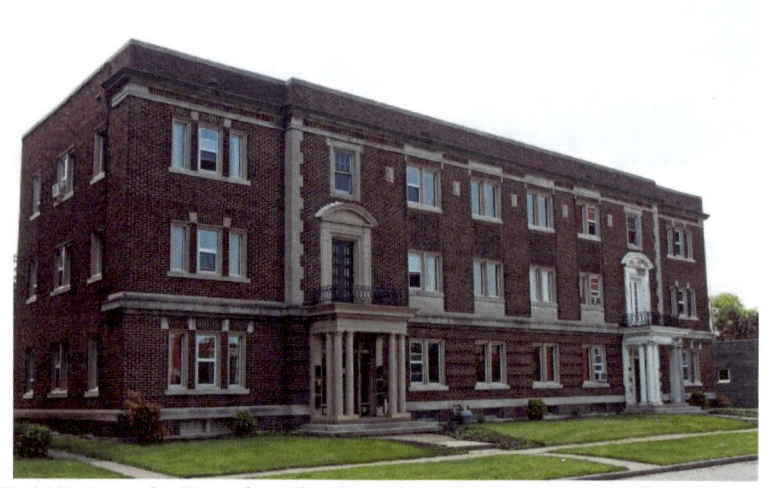

625-645 Argyle Road - The Renfrew Apartment Block – stone belt courses interrupted by columned portals surmounted by Palladian-inspired windows and iron-railed balconettes

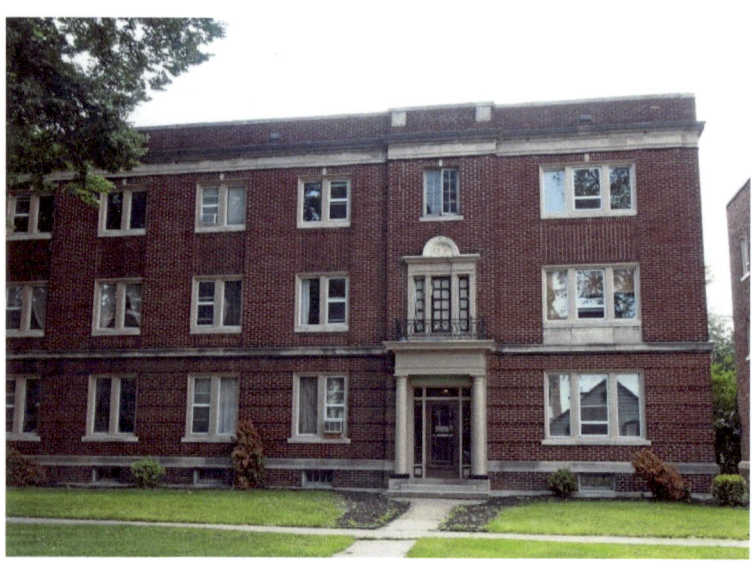

657-693 Argyle Road – The Argyle Apartment Block

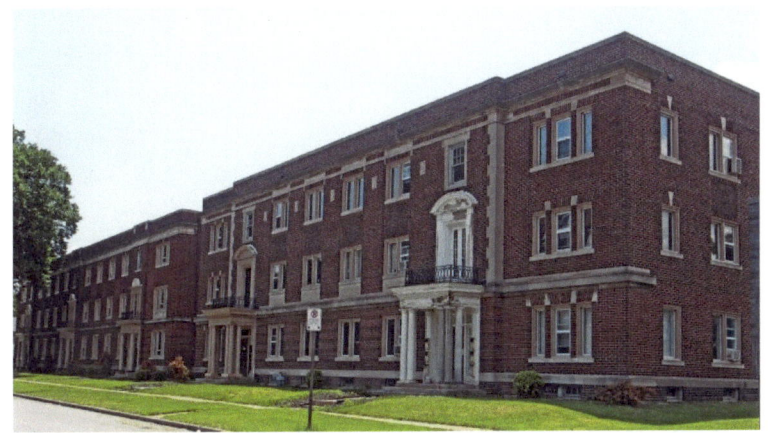

Argyle Road

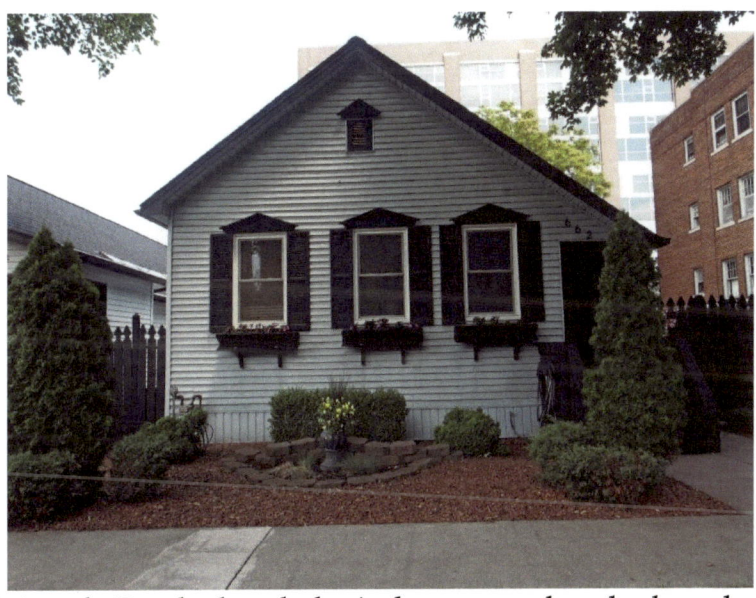

662 Argyle Road – hooded windows, wooden clapboard, side
entrance – c. 1880

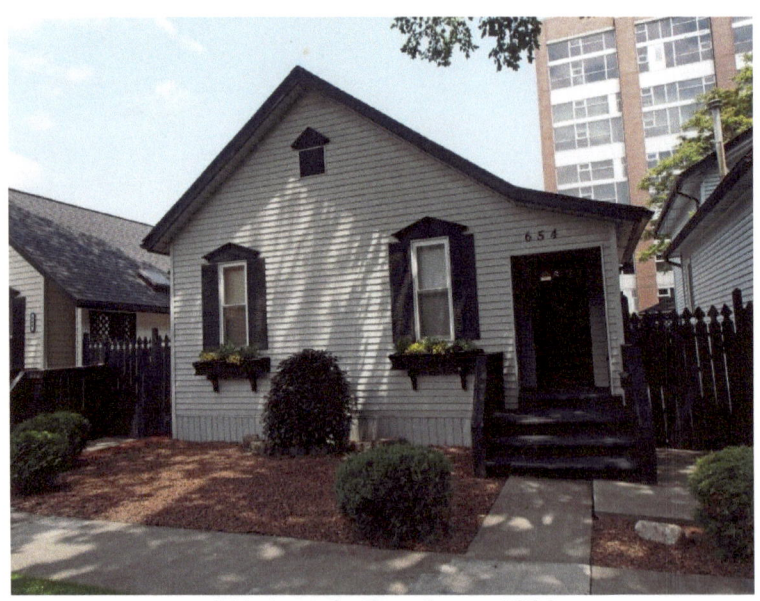

654 Argyle Road – c. 1880

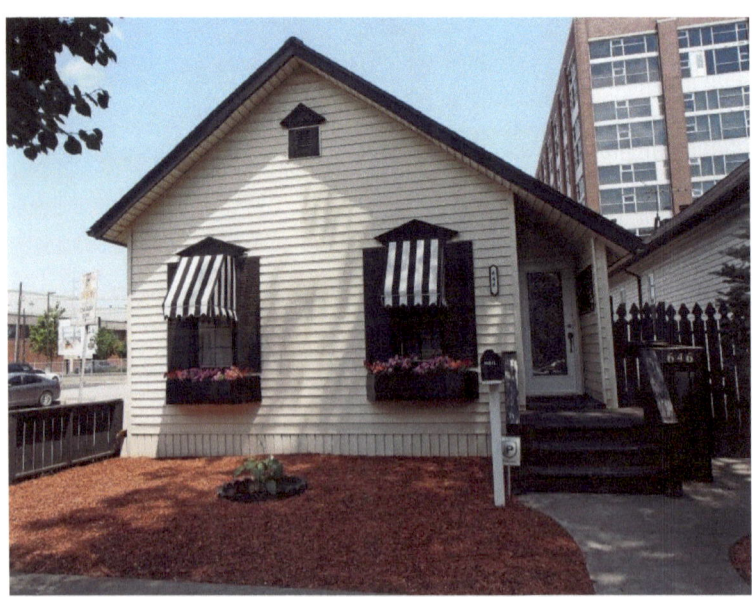

646 Argyle Road – c. 1880

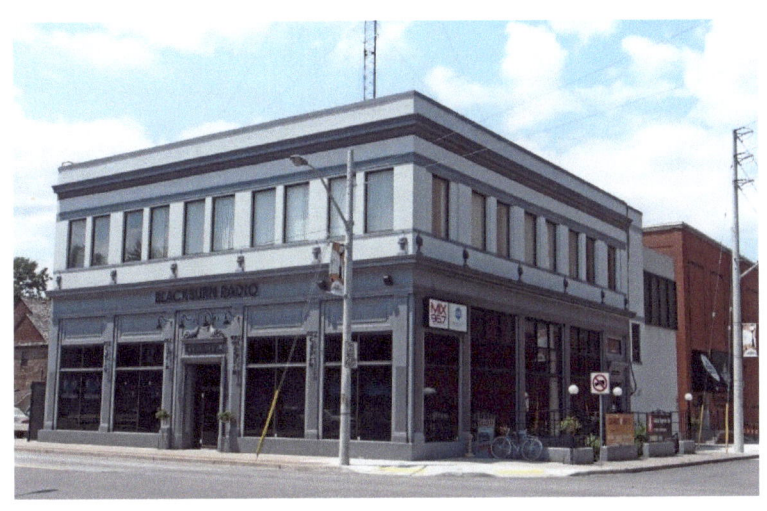

Wyandotte Street East

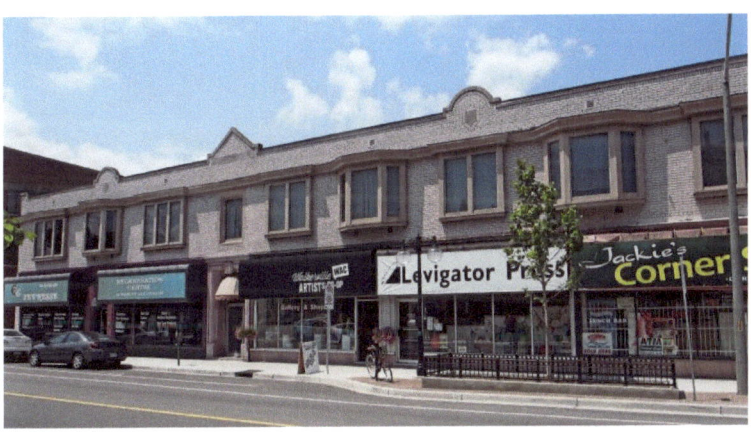

1958-1998 Wyandotte Street East - The Strathcona Block – 1907
Two-storey brick building with timber framed oriel windows,
decorative gables

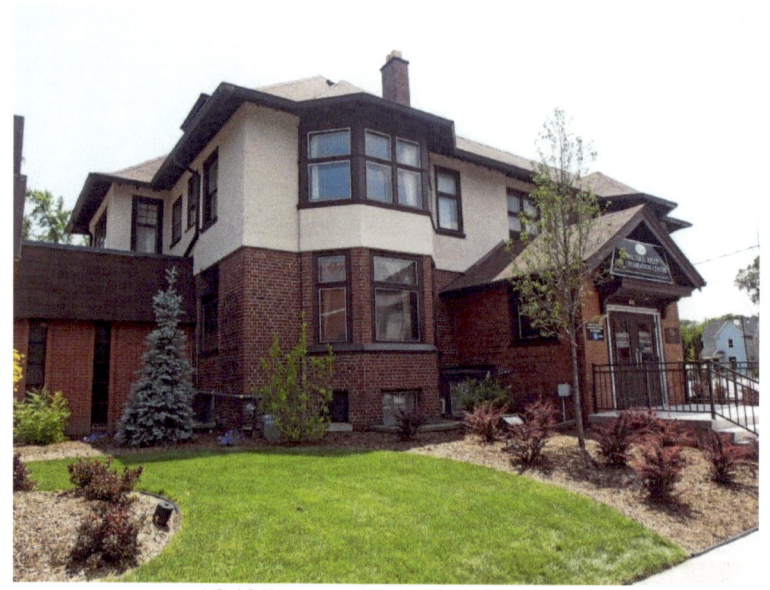

1969 Wyandotte Street East

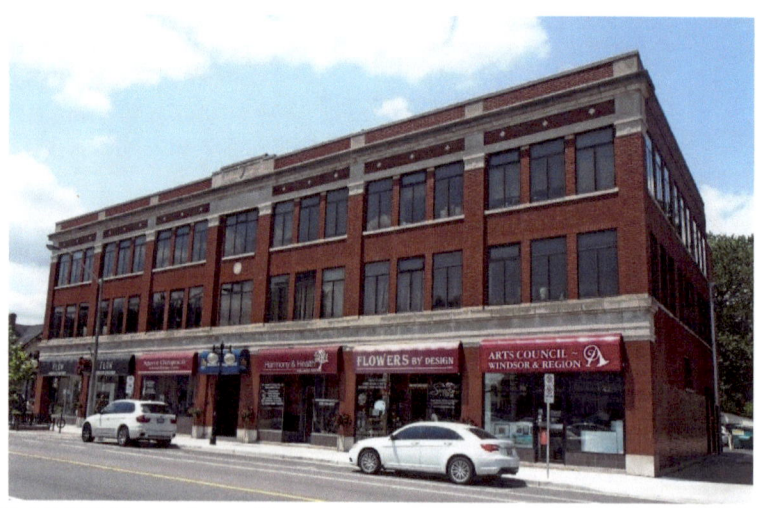

1900-1942 Wyandotte Street East – The Imperial Building 1922

Architectural Terms

Belt Courses: a continuous row of stones set in the wall Example: Argyle Road, see Page 48	
Bay Window: A window that projects out from a wall, in a semicircular, rectangular, or polygonal design. Used frequently in Gothic and Victorian designs. Example: 1969 Wyandotte Street East, see Page 52	
Capital: The uppermost finish or decoration on a column. An Ionic column has a small base, a thin elegant shaft, and a capital composed of volutes which are carved whirls or twists that take the form of a scroll. Example: 415 Devonshire Road, see Page 8	
Cornice Return: decorative element on the end of a gable. Example: Willistead Crescent, see Page 31	
Dentil Moulding: an even series of rectangles used as ornamental decoration in cornices. Example: Willistead Crescent, see Page 31	

Dormer: (French for "sleep") a gable end window that pierces through the plane of a sloping roof surface to create usable space in the top floor or attic of a building by adding headroom. Example: 1948 St. Mary's Gate, see Page 16	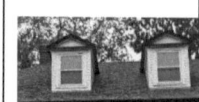
Entrance: The entrance encompasses the doorway and the inner vestibule or, in residential architecture, the covered porch. Example: 712 Devonshire Road, see Page 12	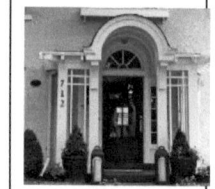
Gable: the triangular portion of a wall between the edges of a sloping roof. Example: see Page 24 **Jacobean Gable:** the gable extends above the roofline Example: 889 Kildare Road, see Page 20	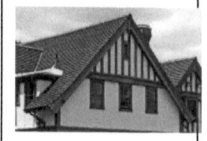 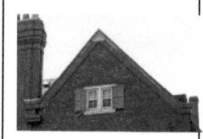

Gambrel Roof: a symmetrical two-sided roof with two slopes on each side; the upper slope is positioned at a shallow angle, while the lower slope is steep. It is similar to a mansard roof, but a gambrel has vertical gable ends instead of being hipped at the four corners of the building. Example: 734 Monmouth Road, see Page 43	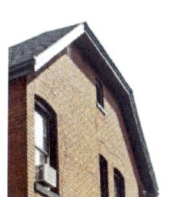
Hipped Roof: a roof where all sides slope downwards to the walls with no gables. Example: 1948 St. Mary's Gate, see Page 16	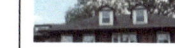
Oriel Window - These small areas were originally set into walls and galleries for the purpose of private prayer. Over time, any projecting window or area on an upper floor was called an oriel. Example: 2026 Willistead Crescent, Page 35	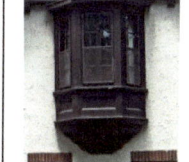
Palladian Window: a large window that is divided into three sections with the centre section larger than the two side sections and usually arched. Example: 841 Kildare Road, see Page 17	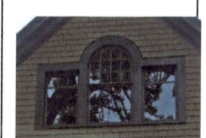
Pediment: a triangular section above the horizontal structure (entablature), typically supported by columns. The inside of the triangle is called the tympanum. Example: 415 Devonshire Road, see Page 8 **Burst Pediment:** Example: Willistead Crescent, see Page 30	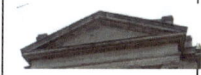 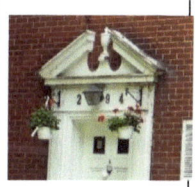

Pilaster: a slightly projecting column built into or applied to the face of a wall for additional structural support. Example: 420 Devonshire Road	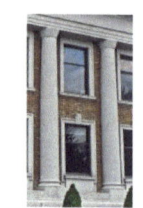
Quoin: masonry blocks at the corner of a wall, often a decorative feature, usually larger or of a different colour than the rest of the wall. Example: 350 Devonshire Road, see Page 7	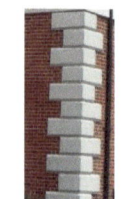
Sidelight: a window, usually with a vertical emphasis, that flanks a door, and is often used to emphasize the importance of a primary entrance. **Transom Window:** the light above the doorway, also called a fanlight. Example: 2017 Richmond Street, see Page 27	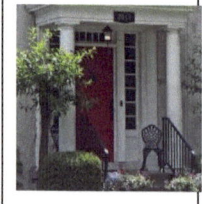
Window Hood: A **hood** is the piece found above window openings, usually of an ornate design, and covers the top third of the opening. Hoods are commonly placed above arched or curved openings on both windows and doors. Example: 662 Argyle Road, see Page 49	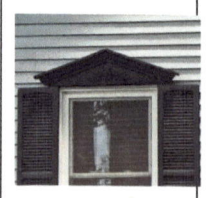

Building Styles

Arts and Crafts: The house was based on the function of the house with rooms oriented to take advantage of the movement of the sun for warmth and light during daylight hours. Side entrances allowed for useable space on the front facade for light or garden use. Arts and Crafts houses have many of these features: wood, stone or stucco siding; low-pitched roof; wide eaves with triangular brackets; exposed roof rafters; porch with thick square or round columns; stone porch supports; exterior chimney made with stone; open floor plans with few hallways; many windows, some with stained or leaded glass; beamed ceilings; dark wood wainscoting and moldings; built-in cabinets, shelves, and seating. Arts & Crafts drew its inspiration from a variety of early picturesque styles, adapting them to modern construction methods. Example: 712 Devonshire Road, see Page 12	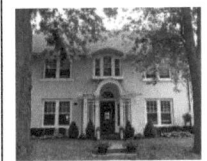
Classical Greek - For the three centuries after the sixth century B.C., the Greeks created monumental buildings with columns, pediments, entablatures, capitals, and bases. Example: 415 Devonshire Road, see Page 8	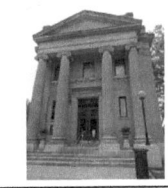

Classical Revival (1820 - 1860) – This style was an analytical, scientific, and dogmatic revival based on intensive studies of Greek and Roman buildings, concerned with the application of Greek plans and proportions to civic buildings. Schools, libraries, government offices, and most other civic buildings were built in the Classical Revival style. The white columned porches of the Classical Revival domestic buildings are identified with the mansions of wealthy land owners in Canada. Example: Devonshire Road, see Page 7	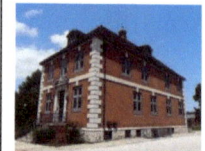
Edwardian, 1900-1930 – This style bridges the ornate and elaborate styles of the Victorian era and the simplified styles of the 20th century. Balanced facades, simple roof lines, dormer windows, large front porches, and smooth brick surfaces are its characteristics. Example: 841 Kildare Road	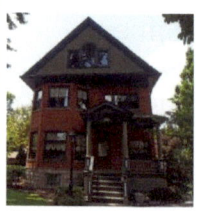
An English country house is a large house or mansion usually unfortified. Example: 1899 Niagara Street, Willistead Manor, see Page 21	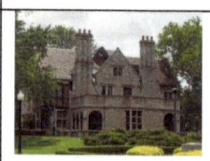
Georgian, before 1860 – This style began with the British King Georges in the 18th century. These buildings have balanced facades around a central door, medium-pitched gable roofs, and small paned windows. Example: 2017 Richmond Street, see Page 27	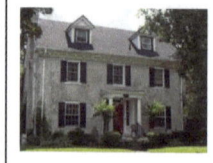

Gothic Revival, 1830-1890 – These decorative buildings have sharply-pitched gables with highly detailed verge boards, pointed-arch window openings, and dichromatic brickwork. It is a common style in Ontario. Example: 1983 St. Mary's Gate – St. Mary's Anglican Church, see Page 15	
Italianate, 1850-1900 – It has wide-bracketed eaves, belvederes, wrap-around verandahs. Example: 833 Kildare Road	
Neocolonial (also Colonial Revival, Georgian Revival or Neo-Georgian) architecture seeks to revive elements of architectural style of American colonial architecture of the period around the Revolutionary War which drew strongly from Georgian architecture of Great Britain. Architecture from the 18th and early 19th centuries in Ontario includes a wide assortment of detailing and ornament applied to a design centered around the fireplace and the source of water. Structures are typically two stories, have a symmetrical front facade with elaborate front doorways, often with decorative crown pediments, fanlights, and sidelights, symmetrical windows flanking the front entrance, often in pairs or threes, and columned porches. Example: 2014 Willistead Crescent, Page 33	

Romanesque Revival, 1880-1910 – This style hearkens back to medieval architecture of the 11th and 12th centuries with a heavy appearance, blocky towers and rounded arches. Example: 546-548 Devonshire Road, see Page 10	
Tudor Revival – exposed timbers with stucco infill, multi-paned windows. Example: 2033 Niagara Street, see Page 24	
Vernacular/Traditional Mode 1638 - 1950 Influenced but not defined by a particular style, vernacular buildings are made from easily available materials and exhibit local design characteristics. Example: 511 Devonshire Road, see Page 9	

www.ingramcontent.com/pod-product-compliance
Lightning Source LLC
Chambersburg PA
CBHW040851180526
45159CB00001B/384